"These reflections on the approach of death, written in the first person, are faithful, biblical, and honest. Although each is accompanied by a text and a closing prayer, these brief devotions do not preach so much as share the apprehension and the hope common to us all. Marilyn McEntyre offers the love of God — and her own heart — to all who wish to receive. This book will prove a faithful companion on what for many is a long journey."

— RICHARD LISCHER
author of *Stations of the Heart:*
Parting with a Son

"A sensitive and helpful encouragement to those living life at its closure — and to living it with openness, faithfulness, and hope. Beautifully done."

— HAROLD G. KOENIG
Duke University Medical Center

"This quietly graceful and grace-filled book allows us the extraordinary, perhaps even unique, privilege of listening in on the thoughts of someone trying to live her dying days mindfully, faithful to herself, to those she loves, to reality, and to God. . . . McEntyre's entirely believable 'channeling' of the dying one's voice is a gift for which I am immensely grateful; this book will stay by my side as I and those dear to me move toward our own farewells."

— MARGARET E. MOHRMANN
author of *Medicine as Ministry:*
Reflections on Suffering, Ethics, and Hope

"Marilyn McEntyre's remarkable meditations on terminal illness manage to be both refreshingly frank and deeply faithful. She knows whereof she speaks, accurately identifying the whole gamut of emotions and experiences that people encounter as they face a death they know is approaching. Startlingly real and profound in hope, this book is a gift to the terminally ill and pastors who would minister to them — and to all of us born to die."

— MICHAEL L. LINDVALL
author of *A Geography of God:
Exploring the Christian Journey*

"In accompanying the dying, McEntyre has come to know the myriad moments that mark the dying process. Her short reflections speak to over fifty facets of this journey in poignant and peace-filled prose. Accompanying prayers provide words for the dying to lean into, especially in moments when their own voice falters. *A Faithful Farewell* should prove equally helpful for family members, friends, chaplains, physicians, and other caregivers. All who walk with the dying in their final days should have a copy of this invaluable book."

— M. THERESE LYSAUGHT
*Institute of Pastoral Studies,
Loyola University Chicago*

MARILYN CHANDLER MCENTYRE

A FAITHFUL
FAREWELL

living your last chapter with love

WILLIAM B. EERDMANS PUBLISHING COMPANY

GRAND RAPIDS, MICHIGAN / CAMBRIDGE, U.K.

Published 2015 by

Wm. B. Eerdmans Publishing Co.

2140 Oak Industrial Drive N.E., Grand Rapids, Michigan

49505

Library of Congress Cataloging-in-Publication Data

McEntyre, Marilyn, 1949-

A faithful farewell: living your last chapter with love /
Marilyn McEntyre.

pages   cm

ISBN 978-0-8028-7260-9 (pbk.: alk. paper)

1. Death — Religious aspects — Christianity.   I. Title.

BT825.M355   2015

236′.1 — dc23

2014047779

www.eerdmans.com

This book is dedicated with awe and gratitude
to those whose dying has taught me not to be afraid,
but to approach the great mystery of our going with
confidence and hope. It has been a privilege to walk
with them in the final days of their journeys.

And to John and our children and their families,
who give me ample reason to linger long
and gratefully in this life.

Whether in life or in death, we are the Lord's.
ROMANS 14:8

CONTENTS

DEALING WITH DYING

Some of us imagine that a merciful death is a swift one: no prolonged suffering, no time for fear, no pain of impending loss, no bearing the burden of others' grief. One blow and it's over. But we really have no way of knowing whether such a transition is more desirable than a gradual dying. And even if we could make that judgment, we don't generally get to choose the manner and time of our own death.

We live longer now, and many of us die more slowly. Medicine and medical technologies keep us alive in ways that introduce uncomfortable ethical ambiguities. We have choices our parents didn't have about treatment and care, including choices about how much of our care to consign to professionals and how to protect the intimacy and privacy of dying in the midst of loving people who gather to see us home.

This book is written for you who are facing that second kind of death. You know there is no likely cure for your condition. You may continue to pray for a miracle of healing, but you also know that healing is bigger than cure, and that it doesn't always mean prolonging this life. You know that illness and death bring new spiritual needs and enforce a different kind of hope.

And you know, as you live through this slow leave-taking, that dying involves a variety of difficulties, uncertainties, adjustments, and surprises. You have numerous things — physical, emotional, and spiritual — to deal with. I've tried to identify and address some of those in these short reflections and prayers: discouragement, embarrassment, boredom, curiosity, loss of privacy, opportunities for new conversations, family conflict, indignities, small losses along the way, moments of new awareness, others' mis-cued efforts to help, spiritual torpor, spiritual adventure, sadness, gratitude. Based on the hours I've spent at the bedsides of those who are living their dying, and on reflections about my own aging and death, I have written these pieces in the first person, hoping that will give them an immediacy they might not have otherwise, and make them more a sharing of a common condition than advice from across the chasm that divides health from illness. "We die with the dying," T. S. Eliot writes, and so I believe we do. I hope these pages will affirm a solidarity that makes every dying an opportunity to awaken and open the heart.

Peruse these pages as they seem to address your particular situation. Different reflections may be useful on different occasions. The prayers included at the end of each reading and those that are gathered in the final section are offered as prayers to lean into when finding your own words requires more energy than you have. I wrote them in the hope that they might not only serve you when you are moved to pray, but also serve as my prayers for you who are traveling a stretch of road toward a crossing we will all come to. The lines from hymns that follow the prayers are offered as invitations to recall the many ways that songs and hymns have sustained the life of faith, especially in hard times.

May you know yourself to be surrounded by a company of angels and a loving community of both dead and living as you approach this great transition and prepare for a faithful farewell.

What We Dreaded

So teach us to number our days
that we may get a heart of wisdom.

PSALM 90:12

"I'm sorry. There's really nothing more the doctors can do."
When I hear this, I'm shocked, or afraid, or grim, or numb, or
resigned. Whatever feeling takes over, I know life will never
be the same. I know I'm on the last leg of this journey, and
though my family and friends will walk with me as far as they
are able, I'm coming up to a transition that's mine alone. It's
my turn to do what every one of us gets to do — leave the ones
given me to love, leave the places on earth I've called home,
relinquish the ambitions that fueled my sense of purpose, and
accept the work of conclusion and preparation.

Dying is work, as different for each of us, I imagine, as the
labor of giving birth is different for every woman who bears
new life into the world. "I had seen birth and death," says the
wise man in T. S. Eliot's poem, "but thought they were different." It turns out they are not so different. The process I face
in what is likely to be a gradual and conscious death will no

1

doubt be strenuous, unpredictable, surprising, and scary, and will require all my spiritual resources, which are probably far greater than I think they are. The focus of my prayer life will have to sharpen. Though I've tried to practice the presence of God, I will come into God's presence now with new urgency, heightened eagerness, and also ambivalence and anxiety — and sometimes anger. Whatever my condition when I show up, I have to trust that God will meet me there, providing what I need for each demanding day of this process.

The conversations I need to have now will offer opportunities for a new level of honesty that may bring new intimacy and freedom between me and those I love. Poems and journals I've read that were written in the months and weeks before death often testify to moments of epiphany or deep peace or complete forgiveness. Sometimes such moments come like gifts, as graceful and simple as the soft fall of a leaf. Sometimes they come in dreams.

I know that the Spirit who meets us the very moment we open listening hearts is near and ready. I know that whatever time I have will be time enough. What most deeply needs to happen can happen. There is a biblical wisdom to King Lear's famous line: "Men must endure their going hence, even as their coming hither. Ripeness is all." We come and we go in "the fullness of time."

Since I am among those to whom preparation time is given, I can receive that gift as an invitation to a new level of reflection, a new challenge to focus my remaining energies, and a new understanding of purpose, which has little to do with productivity, achievement, or social roles. This is my time, held within God's time. May I make every day an offering.

Open my heart, Lord, to the guidance of your Spirit as I walk this final stretch on earth. Calm my fears, and equip me as you will for this journey. With every breath, I receive and release. I have received my life from your hand. Help me to release it in gratitude and trust, at your appointed time. Amen.

> *When I walk through the shades of death,*
> *Your presence is my stay;*
> *One word of Your supporting breath*
> *Drives all my fears away. . . .*

Sharing the Bad News

. . . I am about to die, but God will be with you. . . .

GENESIS 48:21

Since hearing the bad news, I have lain awake at night, trying to take it in. I have wept. Even though I suspected it was coming, hearing words like "nothing more" and "progressed too far" and "organ failure" and "a matter of months" sent shock waves through me that have left me weak and trembling.

I believe what faith teaches — that Christ has gone to prepare a place for us, that death is not the end, but a transition to a new life in new relationship to the communion of saints and all the orders of heavenly beings. Relative to that, this short journey on earth really is like the grass that withers and the flower that fades. I believe that when we go home, we'll get a new, wide-angle view of this life and understand how and why it unfolded the way it did. I imagine seeing it whole, somehow, and being able to say, "Oh, so *that's* what it was about!"

Still, it's hard to go. And it's hard to have to announce my going. I need to "gird my loins" for encounters with people who will be devastated. As I face each one, I need to pray for the patience, clarity, and kindness they will require. I know that a few of them will object and want me to get more opinions and seek more treatment options. I know that some of them will dissolve into their own grief, which may cast me back into my own even as I try to comfort them. I know that some of them will offer pious clichés that I'm already finding irritating, even though I stand in greater need of prayer than ever. I know that some of them will back away because illness makes them uneasy and they won't know what to say. And I know that even they and many others, as word gets out, will encircle me with love, prayer, practical help, encouragement, kindness, and casseroles as the days go by. I know that part of what will be given me in this time is a chance to practice gratitude.

So, as word spreads, as it will, by phone and e-mail, my job is to allow myself to be kept in perfect peace, my mind stayed on Christ, and to meet each person's sorrow with generous imagination for what my dying may mean to them. As I prepare for this final transition, they have to prepare for loss. Both are hard. Even for me, it's not altogether easy to judge which of us are the "lucky" ones. I realize that the measure of life's value doesn't lie in its duration; even terms like "untimely" divert us from the truth that our times are in God's hands. What "in due time" means is for God to define.

In life and in death, as Paul says, we are God's — in going and in remaining. May I go, and they remain, in peace.

God of all comfort, I lay aside the weight of my own concerns in this moment and lift up those for whom my death

*will be a painful loss. May this be a time for deepening
their faith and mine, and for enlarging, as well, their experience of human love. Amen.*

> *Thou wilt keep him in perfect peace
> Whose mind is stayed on Thee. . . .*

What Needs Protection

Because he holds fast to me in love, I will deliver him;
I will protect him, because he knows my name.

PSALM 91:14

"You, O LORD, are a shield about me." I need a shield now. I
need protection from things that drain my limited energy. I
tire easily these days. Sometimes I just feel low-spirited and
easily upset. In the middle of an ordinary conversation about
where to relocate my computer, I start to cry. I need time to
go inward, sometimes to find my way back into God's healing
presence, or sometimes just to enter into quiet or to sort out
my own thoughts, confront my own fears, allow myself my
own memories and imaginings. My mind and heart are very
full.

I need protection from well-intentioned visits that feel
more demanding than helpful. I can see from this angle that
being with sick people involves skills and sensitivities not ev-
erybody has — bless their bumbling hearts! One dear woman
from my reading group seems to manage her discomfort by
talking nonstop. Another doesn't quite know what to say, so

she spends long, awkward pauses staring out the window. I need not to have to visit with everyone who comes by with flowers or offers of company or food, kind as they are. I need not to have to generate conversation, or even listen to it, when I'm bone-tired and world-weary.

I need protection from the weight of other people's grief. Some of them don't realize how crushed I feel by their anguish — and even, irrationally, guilty for causing it. The last thing I want for my family and friends is overwhelming sorrow. I can offer a few obvious words of comfort; we can read Psalms together, and the farewell discourses in John; I can point them to my own sources of consolation. But I can't shoulder their burden. It's my turn to prepare for death. It's their turn to prepare for loss. Those tasks are different. I can't do theirs for them any more than they can do mine for me.

I need protection from the demons that assail me in the night — from fear of death, pain, and mental confusion, from fear of abandonment during my illness, fear of the indignities of dying, fear of the unknown that even my faith doesn't entirely dispel. God of all mercy, protect me.

The words of the old Baptist hymn are good ones to hold onto when fear threatens my peace of mind: "No storm can shake my inmost calm/while to that Rock I'm clinging./Since love is Lord of heaven and earth,/how can I keep from singing?" I love that hymn. It reminds me of the Psalmist's return to song in the midst of trials: ". . . you have been my help, and in the shadow of your wings I will sing for joy." Sadness and sorrow are inevitable; they're with me every day. But if I let them, perhaps they can turn me toward God, who meets us even in the depths of Sheol. Lord, you are my strength and my song. Help me sing a new song in the days to come: make even my lamentations acceptable, and turn my fears into confidence even as I speak them into your listening ear.

You alone, O Lord, make me dwell in safety. Be my refuge and my strength in every trial, every danger, and every challenge of the coming days. At the day's end, make me lie down in peace and sleep, confident in your care. Amen.

I nothing lack if I am His
And He is mine forever. . . .

Denial Dies Hard

They have ears, but they hear not. . . .

PSALM 115:6

Not everyone in my beloved community is willing to accept the truth. That death is coming, surely and soon, is a fact I think I've faced, but some days even I resort to denial that masquerades as hope. The doctors try hard not to raise false hopes. That must be one of the hardest parts of their work — to stand by the bad news when patients so desperately want to hear something else — at least a softer, vaguer, more ambiguous version.

I can usually recognize and redirect my own lapses into denial: *This isn't really happening to me. Tomorrow I'll get up and do a few chores. In another week or two, I'll get out and tend to the garden. If I lie here patiently enough, I'll get well.* I know better. I know that even prayer for a miracle, though permitted, isn't often granted in the simple, literal way it's asked. I know that as the disease progresses, my systems will shut down, and I will shed this body as surely as I left the womb when the time came to leave it.

But when my dearest, most loyal friend starts indulging in denial, it's harder to confront. I see in her desperate gaiety something of her own fear of death, fear of loss, fear of sinking into depression or spiritual darkness. She "needs" me to recover. She "needs" to believe there's something more to be done. She clings to the metaphor of battle because she needs to believe there's a victory to be won over this disease, and that my failing body is occupied territory that can be reclaimed. But those tired metaphors don't help me; they're inaccurate and troubling — to me, at least. I'm too tired to think of my body as a battlefield, or of self-care as a military campaign.

I'm also too tired to play along with the polite deceptions of people who walk in, try to mask their shock at the physical changes they see, and insist that I'm "looking great." I'm not. What they don't understand is that there is a certain relief to be had in accepting even the hardest truths. No pretense, no avoidance, no dancing around the elephant in the room.

What helps me most, when I can do it, is to relax into God's hands and relinquish all effort to make things different from what they are. I accept the day, my coming death, my moods, my thinning, weakening body, and my utter dependence on the love of those whom God has given me to depend on. And I accept my complete reliance on God's own love, which — it consoles me to remember — is "broader than the measures of the mind."

God of truth, help me and those who love me to face what is true. Teach me a hope that harbors no illusions and an acceptance that is bigger and more joyful than resignation.

All that I am and have is yours. I release myself into your loving hands. Amen.

Open wide Thine arms of love:
Lord, I'm coming home. . . .

Losing Control

. . . for [God's] power is made perfect in weakness.

2 CORINTHIANS 12:9

As the medical supplies pile up in the bedroom and bathroom
— the walker and the portable commode and the bedpan, the
catheter and the waterproof mattress pad — I dread every
loss of function and control. I dread the shame even more
than the discomfort and inconvenience. I dread the exposure.
More people have access to my body now. More people touch
me, and in more places than I'm comfortable being touched.
I know that social protocols change with illness, and I know
that increasing dependence on others for personal care is part
of what I have to accept, but I still struggle with feelings of vul-
nerability and shame. Even as I try to protect it, it's hard to love
my failing body, though it has served me well for many years.

One way to come to terms with all this exposure and dependence is to reconsider what it means to "become like a
little child." Although the most common reading of Jesus' admonition to become like little children is to see them in terms
of their trust, open-heartedness, and guilelessness, they're
also unselfconsciously dependent on others for their care

and feeding. Children are recipients. Well-behaved children learn to express gratitude, but even the ungrateful ones have a healthy understanding that they are not in charge, that someone else will take over when they don't know what to do, and that there is safety, not shame, in being cared for. Being cared for is the first — and last — practice of living in community.

The Amish teach that the sick, the elderly, and the dying are gifts to the community because of the love and care they bring forth. That's a beautiful and generous way to think about what my "contribution" may be now to a community in which I used to be much more "useful." Allowing others to be generous and tender, giving them occasion for the sacrifices of time and energy that deepen their investment in my life, may seem like a necessary evil, but perhaps it's a necessary good. I am still a participant. And I cling to the poet Wendell Berry's helpful observation: "Love changes, and in change is true." The way they love me, and I them, has to change. May God help us all accept these changes with grace and kindness.

Gracious God, my help in time of trouble, teach me to accept help with grace. Dispel my shame and bring, in its place, peace, patience, and gratitude for those who minister to me. Let me recognize your loving touch in theirs.

I am weak, but Thou art strong. . . .

Am I a Fighter?

And they shall beat their swords into ploughshares. . . .

ISAIAH 2:4

It's surprising to me how many people have tried to encourage me in the course of this illness by assuring me that I'll get through it because I'm "a fighter." I'm not, really. I can hold my own in an argument, even with a doctor, but I don't aspire to fight. I think of myself as a pacifist, at least by inclination. I avoid conflict; I tried very hard to teach my kids to negotiate rather than pummel each other over their differences; I often find peace of mind in relaxing my rather too firm grip on my own point of view. I know there are times to fight (as the writer of Ecclesiastes might put it) and times to acquiesce with grace. I believe that these days I'm living in the latter.

Of course life is worth fighting for, and I've done due diligence in my "battle" with illness, if one must use that language to describe the arduous process of trying to regain life and health in time of bodily devastation. I've taken all the medications and treatments prescribed, consulted specialists, tried acupuncture, improved my diet, rested, changed my habit of squandering energy, and prayed for healing. Physical healing has not come, and I think it's time to submit to the terms I've been given, the body I've been given, the course of the illness that is now a big part of my story, and, it seems, the way my earthly story will end.

A few folks I love want me to fight harder, try harder, to insist and resist where I still can. It grieves and sometimes angers me that they think I'm "giving up" or "giving in" too soon. There's always one more thing to try. There are heroic measures. There are desperate measures. But I've long since signed the advance health-care directive declining them.

What I'd like, in the time that remains, is to focus on going with gentleness and grace, learning, if I can, a new level of trust in the One who meets me in the midst of my suffering and leads me home. It may be that for me, at this time in my life, being a peacemaker means being willing to stop the fighting and to rest in the peace that passes understanding.

Lord, make me a vessel and an instrument of peace. Let me not cling too tightly to this life as you teach me to let go. Help me to go in peace, and let others, also, go their ways in the perfect peace only you can teach. Amen.

> *The strife is o'er, the battle done;*
> *The victory of life is won;*
> *The song of triumph has begun: Alleluia!*

Privacy

*But when you pray, go into your room and shut the door
and pray to your Father who is in secret. . . .*

MATTHEW 6:6

Whose business is this? The other day I almost asked that
question, and not too kindly, when a particularly inquisitive
neighbor came by for more of an update on my mental and
physical condition than I wanted to deliver. What I have a
right to keep to myself has never been a simple matter for
me, since I believe that we're called into community and that
we are in a deep and real way members of one body: I believe
that, at some level, my business really is others' business. I
know that my death will affect wide circles of people, from
those whose daily lives I share to those who have to do with
me in ways I'm not even aware of. Even my nosy neighbor.

I can't keep my illness private; the grapevine works fast,
and people want to know and share their feelings and pool
information. I can't keep my pain entirely to myself, since
others witness it, and the kind of pain I'm living with in the
end stages of this illness awakens people's natural and kindly

desire to extend comfort. But their efforts to comfort sometimes feel like interrogation: "Where does it hurt? How bad is it? How long has it been hurting like that? Have you told the doctor about it? What helps? Can I help? Would this music/food/poem/distracting sitcom help?" And so on.

I can choose to whom to reveal my last wishes, my anxieties, my prayers, my practical concerns. I need to honor my own instincts about what conversations need to happen, and with whom. But I also know that confidences raise diplomatic concerns. Even legitimate secrets can fuel jealousies among those who want to be close to me. Oddly, sometimes the person I most want to talk with about intimate matters is a stranger — a chaplain, a hospice nurse, or another caregiver who happens to be particularly gifted at listening and receiving unedited thoughts. Not so oddly, some of the folks closer to me wonder why they're not the chosen confidantes.

It's interesting that Jesus wasn't egalitarian in his relationships with the disciples. Some were singled out and some barely mentioned in the Gospel accounts, though no doubt they were all deeply loved. Chosenness is a core biblical idea. And as we are chosen, we are also given choice. As I try to honor my own sense of who should be invited beyond the bedroom door, or whom to call on for help with difficult personal care, or with whom to share my midnight reflections, I can also pray for those I need to keep at greater distance for now. Some people who love me disturb my peace. Some burden me with their own displays of emotion. Some don't listen well, and tire me with their talk. I not only get to choose — I *need* to choose in order to keep my balance and focus on the task before me.

The challenge for me is to model for others, who will have their own turn to die, something of how to die with integrity, kindness, and an open heart — how to offer the "faithful farewell" I'd like to leave them with. So I will rest when I need rest, and keep the door closed to all who might disturb it. I will ask for help from those who are most helpful, and try to receive generously from others, but only when I have the energy to do so. And I will try to temper self-protection with gratitude, praying that I will be able to accept with grace the intentions of those who want to come in close and say their farewells.

Jesus, I remember your solitary sojourns in the desert, and how often you withdrew from those you loved to pray. Teach me when to send others away, and how to take my leave of all who love me in ways that honor both my needs and theirs. Amen.

Now to be Thine and Thine alone,
O Lamb of God, I come, I come. . . .

Clinical Encounters

. . . and though she had spent all her living on physicians, she could not be healed by anyone.

LUKE 8:43

Apparently medical care is the number-one cause of bankruptcy among Americans — a fact that strikes me as scandalous and fills me with sorrow. That I have insurance is a comfort. But that so many still struggle, even after tentative reforms, to pay their medical bills makes me painfully aware of my privilege.

I don't think it's only patients who suffer from the inadequacies of the health care system. The doctors, nurses, orderlies, dieticians, social workers, and other staff who roam the halls of the hospital, cheerful and kind as most of them are, seem to me to be working under constraints that severely limit what must be most satisfying about their work. Some of them would like to spend a few more minutes with me, but don't have them to spend. I imagine they look at me and see some reminder of the dying in their own families — parents, perhaps, or beloved grandparents, or siblings who died far too soon. The young ones may still feel a bit fearful and awkward about ministering to the dying, since they have been trained and conditioned to think of themselves as healers. No one really wants death to happen here.

As I lie here receiving their dutiful attentions, I have begun to wonder how I can minister to them. I can ask questions — one each visit, perhaps — about their children, their weekends, their research projects, their reading. I can weave prayers around their answers. I can practice acceptance, patience, good humor, candor, clarity, and faith. I can find ways to share with them what sustains me — a hymn line, a Bible verse, a poem, a prayer.

I can also offer them what I hope for from caregivers — compassion, empathy, humane recognition that we share the terms all living beings are given when they enter this life — the bodies that are our teachers, the fallible senses, the risks, the losses, the capacity for unexpected pleasure even in dark times. I can pay attention to the ones that seem particularly in need of an encouraging word. I can complain, if at all, only about what they have some authority or ability to address. I can laugh. Everyone here is in need of laughter. Some days it is the best way to bestow blessing.

Lord of all life, help me to connect with all those who care for me in a way that will leave them feeling cared for. Keep my heart open even as my energies and organs fail. Make my living and dying an offering of love. Amen.

We meet you, O Christ, in many a guise:
Your image we see in simple and wise. . . .

Pain

If I speak, my pain is not assuaged,
and if I forbear, how much of it leaves me?

JOB 16:6

"On a scale of one to ten, how much does it hurt?" This non-sense question doctors like to ask doesn't give me either words or images for the pain I'm in, or a strategy for dealing with it. Sometimes it seems more than I can bear. Is it a ten, or simply "off the charts"? Sometimes it's bearable, but I still want and need immediate relief. Is that a six? I answer the question (after politely pointing out what a crude instrument of assessment it is) because it's asked, but it leaves me wondering how to live with pain that may be partially abated, but isn't likely to go away altogether.

Job tells the truth about persistent pain. I'm not too interested in putting on a happy face. I'm interested in finding a way to tell and live what is true about bodily suffering, and finding some strategy that allows it to help my spirit grow toward God, not feed on resentment or fear. This may be a good time to reread Job, remembering it's a story not as much about rescue as about divine encounter. And it's about faithfulness that endures through the hardest trials because, though the ways of God may be incomprehensible, God is also our refuge and our strength.

If nothing else, physical pain is certainly a reminder of the contingency of physical life. Faith gives me assurance that ultimately we won't have to live on these terms, in physical bodies that are susceptible and frail and wired for pain signals that can be very hard to silence. But the promise of life in another condition doesn't alleviate present pain. My belly hurts. My neck hurts. My back hurts from so much time in bed. It hurts to sleep on my side.

I try what I can. I pray. I practice slow breathing. I imagine myself riding a wave when the pain crests. I find a place in my mind from which I can observe it with a certain detachment. I speak words of affirmation to God, who holds me in these hard hours. "This is my body. This is my body. This is my body." Or "Jesus, be with me." Or "I accept what I must. I ask for release." Repetition helps. Sometimes holding a physical thing — a cross, a smooth stone, a squeeze ball, a willing hand — helps ground the flailing energies that make me frantic with pain. I see why people pray with beads: they keep body and spirit linked when it feels as though the body is reeling off on its own crazed trajectory.

I accept pain relievers when they're given. I ask for what I need. Sometimes I badger my caregivers for more. And sometimes I just turn into my pillow and beg for sleep. In all of these efforts I'm trying to reclaim Jesus' promise to be with me always — always — and imagine as I close my eyes on the light that hurts them that I am held gently by the One whose light never hurts me, who knows my pain better than anyone else, and who needs no explanation.

Merciful God, relieve my pain. And in those hours when there is no relief, hold me in your strong embrace and give me the fortitude to bear it. I ask for patience and strength and trust in this trying time. I rest in your great love. Amen.

O Lord, hold my hand while I run this race. . . .

Unhelpful Help

. . . be patient in tribulation, be constant in prayer.

ROMANS 12:12

I know this verse in Romans well. But it's hard to be patient with caregivers who seem rushed or mechanical or too busy to listen, or who hurt me when they could be more gentle. I need them to know how to help me turn over without reawakening nausea, and how to help me stand up without pulling me. I feel physically and emotionally vulnerable, and at others' mercy. I need them to know how to do their jobs.

Some do their jobs better than others. Some doctors are kinder. Some nurses take the extra minute or two to deadhead the flowers on the nightstand or relay a good story. Some of those whose work it is to do simple, practical things like cleaning come in with a quiet that is a gift in itself. Others don't seem to realize that they're disrupting hard-won sleep with rattling equipment. In a general — and real — way, I'm grateful for their care. I'm certainly aware of how many are dying with no one to care for them. But in more specific and immediate ways, I feel annoyed or insulted or frustrated when caregivers don't seem to care quite enough to pay attention.

I'm probably not going to be among those at whose funeral people say, "I never heard her complain." I'm not sure I even want to be. Sometimes well-placed complaints help prevent continuing incompetence or identify problems in the health care system or give caregivers useful information about how to handle a body in pain. I've always thought it's a citizen's or consumer's or parent's duty to complain. It's part of the job description.

As long as life lasts, learning can happen. This seems to be a time to learn the difference between abject submission to ineptitude and the real patience that engages with others kindly at the level of their intentions. Perhaps it's a time to learn to complain more thoughtfully. Perhaps it's a time to practice a cheerful assertiveness in the service of honesty. It's certainly a time to remember how Jesus, in the course of his very public life and very painful death, had moments when he called careless people sharply to account as well as moments when he submitted not only to incompetence but to radical injustice. Once again I realize that the hope of becoming in some way "Christ-like" brings me to paradox and discernment.

May I recognize when it is time to complain and when it is time to hold my peace and make my peace with this public and disorderly process of dying.

Jesus, teach me now how to accept what others have to offer in the spirit in which it is offered. Help me to know when to ask for adjustments and when to put up with others' imperfections, knowing so well my own. Help me to be both clear and kind in all my dealings with those who offer me their help. Amen.

> *Help us accept each other*
> *As Christ accepted us;*
> *Teach us as sister, brother,*
> *Each person to embrace. . . .*

Anger

Be angry and do not sin; do not let the sun go down on
your anger.

EPHESIANS 4:26

I'm tired of being a good sport. I'm tired of exhorting myself
to patience. I'm tired of being a good patient. At the moment
I'm not even attracted to the notions of saintliness or heroism
that inspired me when I was a kid reading Bible stories and
biographies. I don't want this illness — or the pain or the
inconvenience or the disappointment or the wracking tears
that come in the night. I don't want my family's sadness. It all
feels unfair, untimely, and ungodly. Much as I've been taught
that pain and death are part of life, that God is with us in all
of it and meets us there, I'm having a hard time finding God
in the fog of loss, and I'm pretty tired of looking.

Some nights, fury comes like a sudden wind and whips
through my body, leaving every nerve on edge. I may have
started the day in hope and good humor and laughed or cried
or exchanged hugs with sweet friends who came by. But then
darkness descends and, if I have any impulse to turn to Scrip-

ture or prayer, it's the Psalmist's imprecations or Job's outrages I seek out. Sometimes I just reach for the remote and watch the most escapist movie I can find.

I've heard the answers that pastors and theologians and wise teachers give to the great "Why" questions, but it's impossible not to ask them. Why do we have to suffer? Why do I have to suffer? Why death? Why now? Why in this way?

When I'm awash in these railings, I can't really pray. Others have to do that for me. My heart is full of a kind of anger that makes me reach for an old word like wrath. It burns loud, and it's consuming. When it's ignited, it is fearful. Though it's "mine," I'm afraid of it myself.

But I may not need to be. Anger comes and goes, and somehow I weather it, and love eventually absorbs or dilutes or detoxifies it. Sometimes that love comes from a patient person at my bedside, sometimes by direct infusion, like cold water poured into my burning heart.

I suppose some anger is a necessary release. I remember Maya Angelou's helpful distinction: "Bitterness is like cancer. It eats upon the host. But anger is like fire. It burns it all clean." I'm not too sure it always leaves me feeling "clean," but the honesty of anger may prevent more insidious soul-sicknesses — self-pity, false piety, depression, and the bitterness Angelou so rightly mentions as a state of mind and heart more dangerous than anger.

It comes over me unbidden. I can't simply drive it away. Like pain, it may be something to be borne, released as soon as it can be, and reflected upon in tranquility, when that blessed gift, as it always has been, is restored.

Loving God, release me from my anger, or, while it lasts, let it give me energy and direction and forestall the dark depression into which I might sink like quicksand. Turn it to prayer. And may my wrestling with you, like Jacob's, end in blessing. Amen.

> *From every ailment flesh endures*
> *Our bodies clamor to be freed;*
> *Yet in our hearts we would confess*
> *That wholeness is our deepest need.*

Foggy Days

. . . mist and darkness fell upon him. . . .

ACTS 13:11

Confusion is almost worse than pain. Drugs that help also dull the edges of a mind I desperately want to keep clear. Some of them make me feel sluggish and stupid and unable to capture words that seem to float in a fog bank. Sometimes people come to visit, hold my hand, and speak to me as though I'm at the far end of a tunnel, or have regressed to imbecility. Bless them for their efforts. But I find those encounters acutely embarrassing.

Practically speaking, I know I can take advantage of my clearer moments. And I can forewarn those who come in and out about what the drugs seem to do — how they alter the rhythms of my consciousness and energy — and ask them for understanding. I can also ask the doctor to calibrate medications in a way that takes into account both pain relief and preservation of enough clarity to be present to those who love me and to have the conversations I most want before I go.

I can also recognize and accept that confusion is one dimension of the suffering that is given to me now. To be grateful for pain relief is also to accept the tradeoffs it brings as one more of the many ironies of the human condition. This dance with death is not simple. The decisions about medication are sometimes exhausting, sometimes mine to make, sometimes taken out of my hands. What I need to receive and respond to are the grace of the moment, the needs of the moment, and the call of the moment. What I need to accept is that the mind is not separable from the body, and that the work I'm doing at a soul level is not dependent on the vagaries of a befuddled brain.

The work I'm doing is much like the labor of giving birth, which happens, in a sense, in spite of oneself. I am being prepared in ways I cannot control, but can trust. "God will not leave us comfortless," Jane Kenyon reminds us in "Let Evening Come," the lovely poem she wrote as her own death approached. And I can trust that, even in the helplessness of a wandering mind, Jesus' promise that he is with us always serves me now. Not all who wander are lost.

Guide me, God of light, through all the dark passages of this journey. Let my trust in you uphold me when all I see and hear feels uncertain and precarious. Grant me clarity and relief from pain. When I must trade one for the other, grant me confidence in your complete, unconditional love. Amen.

Savior, like a shepherd lead us,
Much we need thy tender care. . . .

Boredom

. . . the world languishes and withers. . . .

ISAIAH 24:4

I expected the pain and the sadness, even some depression, but I didn't expect boredom. I'm not used to being bored. Even in the earlier stages of this illness, my days were full, and life seemed to keep coming at me with new — or old — demands and challenges and amusements. Now that my energy is so diminished, it seems hard to direct what remains of it in ways that either lift me into life-giving engagement or allow me to quiet into reflection or contemplation or prayer. I never thought of boredom as something with a force of its own, but sometimes it seems to override all other impulses — to pray, to think creatively, to imagine what I need from others and ask for it.

Sometimes boredom seems like a kind of depression — either a symptom of depression or a cause of it. The Desert Fathers used the term *acedia* to describe a spiritual state of distraction, boredom, inability to focus one's energies. They often found relief in manual labor, but that recourse isn't really open to me in my present condition. I imagine this is why people knit or crochet or, if a willing visitor is available, play semi-mindless games — and those can certainly help.

Even this rather humble misery may be "given to God," as my mother put it — not simply as a problem to be solved or a pain needing relief, but as a condition to be accepted and transformed. Small practices — focused breathing, simple litanies of willingness or thanksgiving or praise or intercession, noticing the small gifts of the day — can become acts of acceptance.

It may be that the way out of boredom is not to escape into distraction, but to move into it with the intention and prayer that these moments be transfigured by the One whose loving guidance is always available and who understands our humblest, and most irritating, needs.

Jesus, you put up with so many things that must have tried your patience in the years you spent among earthly companions who so often missed your meaning. Grant me patience with boredom, openness to your enlivening Spirit, and trust in the divine love that cares for and about me even in the grayest hours. Amen.

Take Thou our minds, dear Lord, we humbly pray;
Give us the mind of Christ each passing day. . . .

Nausea

A man's spirit will endure sickness, but a crushed spirit who can bear?

PROVERBS 18:14

Jean-Paul Sartre wrote a whole book called *Nausea*. It's hardly an enticing title, but I can imagine why one might want to bring some focus to that particular experience, both literal and metaphorical. It's unlike anything else, and — I'm inclined to think when I'm in it — *worse* than anything else. When I'm riding waves of nausea, it seems worse than pain, though that's one of those pointless comparisons that doesn't bear objective examination.

The claim in Proverbs that sickness is more bearable than a crushed spirit is a helpful reminder when my body becomes such an uncomfortable place to be. Though the sickening waves of reaction to chemotherapies, or simply food are immediately preoccupying, they don't touch the place where the Spirit holds me steady.

Even so, the suffering of nausea makes me fearful. I'm afraid of the next onset. I'm afraid to turn over because the slightest move might trigger it. I'm afraid of what feels like evisceration when the retching seems to have forced everything in me out. *I just can't do this again,* I think to myself. Fear and nausea challenge my authority over my own body, but I've also learned that I can reclaim that authority. I can go into the "observer" or "witness" part of myself and notice what's happening to me without being utterly overtaken by it. Being in that place reminds me of being a child in my dad's arms, feeling secure enough to look out at the barking dog or shuffling crowds in the street, unafraid.

This is a way, I've found, to "live the paradox." It's a kind of "aikido move," as I've come to think of it: relax into the pain, relax into the fear. Don't resist the very thing that assails you, but move into it and find a place from which to notice what's happening. It's a movement from the "small self" who is suffering to the "big self" who quietly observes the events and sufferings of this frail human life from a place of security and peace.

This is the place from which the phrases come that keep me connected to that ultimate security: "Let nothing disturb thee, let nothing affright thee. . . ." "Be not afraid. I am with you always." "This, too, shall pass." And a familiar word of assurance, like a drumbeat, that steadies me in the waves: "You are held. You are witnessed. You are accompanied. You are loved." In these words I take my rest.

Loving God, I know that sickness is part of our plight on this ailing planet. And I know it will come to an end, as this life will, and all things be made new. Refresh me even in the midst of this particular suffering, I pray. Calm me, let your peace suffuse me, body and soul, and let me lie down and sleep in peace, "for you alone, O Lord, make me dwell in safety." Amen.

> *Out of the depths I cry to thee,*
> *Lord God! O hear my prayer!*

The Good Days

. . . and so our God gives light to our eyes and a little relief in our bondage.

EZRA 9:8

I have good days. Inexplicably, some mornings I wake up almost pain-free. Or my anxieties evaporate. Or the awkwardness of eating with the wrong hand strikes me as funny, and I find myself laughing instead of excusing myself.

On good days I find myself awakened to small pleasures like the squirrels' chittering outside the window and the feel of a fresh pillowcase. I listen hard for the sound of kids in the park down the street — especially for the satisfying thwack of a racket on a ball: somehow the memory of a strong swing and the feel in my arm of the ball hitting the sweet spot makes me grateful instead of sad — on the good days.

On good days I enjoy the dubious privilege of surprising my visitors with a little gallows humor. I feel clever and wry when I deliver a bit of inside medical information that unsettles people's ideas of what "feeling better" means.

On good days I remember, too, that I can afford to be kind.

I urge my caregivers to go out for lunch with someone, or see a movie. I take the trouble to write a thank-you note no one expects, with a cartoon figure in the margin. I let someone else pick the evening movie.

On good days, images and phrases from the poems and stories that have equipped me for this journey come back to me and help me. I remember Michael J. Cohen writing, "With infinite wisdom and care your life is constantly sustained. . . ." I remember Gandalf telling Frodo, "All we have to decide is what to do with the time that is given us." And I remember Annie Stenzel, after her diagnosis, concluding a poem about her disease with these remarkable lines:

> . . . let me bless and cherish every moment
> of its absence to arm myself with consciousness
> that every earthly darkness has given way to light,
> thus far.

On good days my appetite for what most deeply sustains me is stirred. I want to hear my favorite Psalms. And then more of them. I want someone to read the whole book of Galatians with me, and the last chapter of Revelation. And a Billy Collins poem. And something deeply funny and real by Flannery O'Connor or Anne Lamott. I savor the quiet of afternoon solitude, and find myself effortlessly at prayer. I listen when I'm there, and I hear (a weak, inadequate verb for what comes in the silence) the voice of the Spirit reminding me that all shall be well, and all manner of thing shall be well, and I am filled with knowing that it is so.

Thank you, God, for the good days. May I bless and cherish them, knowing they will add to the strength I need for the harder ones. Bless those who make them good days, and who remember them in darker times. Let me live in gratitude on good days and bad, and in everything give thanks. Amen.

> *Be this, while life is mine,*
> *My canticle divine:*
> *May Jesus Christ be praised!*

Remembering

Remember the days of old; consider the years long past. . . .

DEUTERONOMY 32:7

Recently I came across some arresting words from Dietrich Bonhoeffer's near-death reflections. Knowing that his young life was soon to be terminated, Bonhoeffer wrote, "I want my life. I demand my own life back. My past. You!" The longing rings true. Which of us would not seize a chance to do it again, and differently — to walk, we think, more faithfully with God as our guide, to live the life of faith we might have lived. Poet Christian Wiman's comment on this outcry seems equally moving and true, coming as it does from a man who has faced his own likely death by cancer for some time: "It takes a moment to realize just how poignant and surprising this longing is. Fear, when you are close to death, can be as much about memory as mortality." What will be the measure of my days? What will they add up to? How will they be judged by others and by God?

How we tell our stories to ourselves and to others can vary

41

widely in emphasis and scope. We can tell them as stories about loss. We can tell them as stories about growth, or discovery, or influences, or grace. There are painful ways to tell my story, and I tend to rehearse it that way in dark times. That's when I want the past back so I can fix it.

"The past is never dead," William Faulkner wrote. "It's not even past." I experience the truth of that curious claim in the relentless durability of conscience: "My sin is ever before me." God may remember our sins no more, but I remember mine rather well. I remember people I've hurt, betrayals large and small, time wasted in pointless distractions, failures of imagination and will.

More than one poet has made a very different claim about the past that brings me a ray of hope in my bleak rememberings: "The past keeps changing." It does indeed. The past changes as I understand more about my own immaturities and inexperience and unmet needs. It changes as my faith and theology deepen. It changes as my family and friends mirror it back to me in their stories — bless them for their re-arrangings and their humor and their forgiveness!

When biblical peoples are admonished to remember their collective story, it is generally in order to see in it a record of God's guidance and mercy and faithfulness. That may finally be the only real point in remembering. My children will remember and perhaps pass on some of my stories insofar as they serve their own purposes. But my own remembering, now, is not to retrieve or revise or even repent, since I've already done that, but to recognize what God has allowed and enabled to happen in my particular human journey. When I shift the focus from what I have done to what God has done for me and in me and by means of me, it is a very different story, and one worth telling.

Author of salvation and witness to our human stories, bless my remembering. In the bleak memories as well as in the happy ones, let me trace the evidence of your divine purposes at work and your hand holding me, then and now, even at the edges of Sheol. Let me receive each remaining moment as a reminder of the newness of life you promise. Amen.

In all the past, through all our hopes and fears,
Thy hand we see. . . .

New Identity

My radiant appearance was fearfully changed, and I retained no strength.

DANIEL 10:8

I remember being an interesting person — a lively conversationalist, a compassionate listener, funny sometimes, always good for an ironic comment on the news and a thoughtful reading in Bible studies. These days almost everyone who visits leads with "How are you?" — a question that's hard to answer medically, and diplomatically complicated, and sends me on a tiresome review of my body's uncomfortable life since yesterday or last week.

I feel as though even those closest to me look at me and see my illness. They want to help, they want to comfort me, they want to be good caregivers — bless their hearts — but they shy away from some of the ordinary give-and-take that friends and family members normally provide, and that I miss. They don't tease me as much, or needle me into new perspectives. They don't share their own problems, no doubt thinking that they pale in comparison to mine. They don't realize that I *want* to hear their problems — they might be a welcome distraction from the incessant self-focus that illness tends to demand.

We're all patients, I want to say to them. As T. S. Eliot dryly reminds us, "The whole world is our hospital." But that's not all we are — and that's not all I am. I'm also a person who's still growing, still capable of a whole spectrum of ordinary feelings — frustration, pleasure, anxiety, amusement — and of deeper ones: longing, sorrow, hope. I don't want our conversation to dry up into one channel; I want it to spread into all the little tributaries of the rich life experience we share.

Health is wholeness, and wholeness opens the way to holiness. So I want wholeness in my relationships if I can't have it in my body. The love and conversation of my friends help make me whole. Healing words are sometimes just ordinary observations about the morning news, movie reviews, musings about kids' behavior, decisions about vacation options.

I don't want to be an object of pity. I'd rather be engaged with life and considered a full participant while I'm living it. Even if my capacity to do ordinary things is diminished, I'd like people to push me a little. I think about Jesus telling the lame man to stand up, pick up his bed, and walk. That man had work to do. And so do I. Even if I can't get up and drag this hospital bed down the block, there are still things I can rise to. I want my friends to help me rise up and lift what I can and walk with them on the stretch of path that remains.

Lord, help me to live each day as fully as I can. Help me to keep noticing, wondering, listening, and opening my heart and mind to what the moment brings. Deepen my friendships and make them durable in ways that help us all endure what we must of sorrow and hang onto the hope we share. Amen.

> Take my moments and my days;
> Let them flow in endless praise. . . .

Ambiguities

Whoever seeks to preserve his life will lose it,
but whoever loses his life will keep it.

LUKE 17:33

I'm thinking about Jesus "setting his eyes toward Jerusalem." He knew what he was facing, and he went forward to meet it. I know what I'm facing at this point, but it's hard some mornings to decide whether to strive to keep living ("fighting," as some insist on putting it) or to give full consent to death, embrace it, and prepare for it.

Those who desperately want me to live a little longer, who love me and will miss me, know my final wishes about health care, and will, despite their sadness, respect them. I would like to continue in this life a little longer for their sake, if not for my own, as long as I'm not in terrible pain. I love life. We're designed to love life. But there's a broad gray area I have to navigate now. Rest, relinquishment of struggle, and peace in the arms of God, whatever that may be like, are an increasingly appealing prospect.

I'm not altogether sure how to think of heaven. Jesus offered a series of metaphors for the kingdom of heaven, each rich with suggestion, all of them ambiguous. It seems hope of heaven has to involve trust that the life we enter after death will involve real relationships with fellow creatures and with God that are joyfully fulfilling and beyond our imagining. I believe that, and still I cling to this life. I don't want to leave it.

As I spend these lengthening hours in bed, it helps me to go through a litany of trust, commending to God's care each beloved person, one by one, praying for deep reassurance that they will be held in that care as they go through their mourning. They will die, as I will, when the time comes, and I see that part of my work now is to confront my death in ways that may encourage them in facing their own. Letting go is a lesson we get over and over, in small ways and larger ones, each time preparing for this last letting-go. As Mary Oliver writes so helpfully, we are all called to "love what is mortal," and "when the time comes to let it go/to let it go."

Jesus, help me to claim and imitate the generous relinquishment you so perfectly modeled. Help all my farewells to be faithful to the love I've been given. Help me to live every day I'm given in gratitude and, when the time comes to let go, to let go in complete trust, floating, weightless and free, into your waiting arms. Amen.

If you get there before I do,
(Coming for to carry me home)
Tell all my friends I'm coming too. . . .

Regrets

As it is, I rejoice, not because you were grieved,
but because you were grieved into repenting. . . .

2 CORINTHIANS 7:9

Every week I have looked forward to the moment when, after the confession, the pastor offers this familiar reassurance:
"Friends, believe the good news: In Jesus Christ, you are forgiven." I rely on that. I rely on God's infinite mercy when my
own checkered past rises up to haunt me. I remember all the
ways I've failed people, neglected them, spoken ill of them;
all the times I've distracted myself when I might have prayed
or returned to a center point of stillness, open-heartedness,
gratitude.

I have in fact, as the old Episcopal confession puts it, "done
those things I ought not to have done, left undone those
things I ought to have done," and there is "no health" in me.
The literal truth of that last acknowledgment in these days of
final illness carries a rather painful irony. I bear in my body
and psyche the marks and scars of a life imperfectly lived and
deep regrets over lost opportunities and the hard fact that we

don't get to erase mistakes and redo the past. I have to accept forgiveness. It's the only release from self-condemnation.

For me, accepting forgiveness isn't altogether simple. I can know I'm forgiven and be truly grateful, but there is still the psychological residue of regret. *I wish I hadn't . . .* that list is a long one. The best thing I can do with it is turn it into a long testimony to God's faithfulness. When I consider all the things I wish I hadn't done, I also see how consistently God has allowed good things to take root and blossom in the rubble of my past. Not only that, but I can see how my story of failures and mistakes is also a story about grace.

These days I need to see and claim my life — a life I have loved living and have tried to live well — in those terms. It is what it is. It is God's now, as it always has been, to transform and turn to divine purposes — even those things I did carelessly, self-servingly, blindly. I release it all into the Light that transforms all it touches. Every time regret comes, I exhale it into that Light with a prayer that even what I have done badly may somehow be turned to blessing.

You who made us out of dust and entered into the muddy business of human living, make my story, with all its subplots and shadows, a gift to those who remember me. Heal my regrets and theirs with a miracle of new seeing, turning brokenness to beauty and bitterness to acceptance. Amen.

> *'Twas grace that taught my heart to fear,*
> *And grace my fears relieved. . . .*

Incompletions

And even now you are not yet ready. . . .

1 CORINTHIANS 3:2

I have a closet full of unfinished projects and a to-do list that, even in illness, I haven't managed to stop worrying about. The old letters I had hoped to winnow and organize and the new letters I should have written, the writing project that never got beyond the first draft, the roses I still love to tend that need pruning, the half-finished painting or quilt or antique repair — these may all have to be left for someone else to finish. This saddens me, though there are bigger things to be sad about. I'd like to tie up the loose strands of my life. I'd enjoy the small closures those completions might afford.

But perhaps incompletion is an avenue of connection. Perhaps those who finish what I have started will discover an outward and visible sign of the communion of saints in sharing my efforts and completing them. Perhaps they will find some consolation — or amusement — in the tasks. Or it may be that what is unfinished will remain unfinished. If that's the case, it's one more chance for me to let go and receive forgiveness. It occurs to me that I've never been to a funeral where someone talked about what the deceased had failed to complete.

I thought I'd learned long ago that what we do is mostly about process, anyway. As John Milton so starkly put it, "God doth not need either man's work or his own gifts." God gives us work to do in this world so we can learn to love, learn to be the Body of Christ. It's all practice. It matters that the hungry be fed and that caring gestures, hospitality, and competent work be enacted. But what finally happens to any of us is in God's hands. It's time to take that bigger perspective now. Not one of us is indispensable. Any one of those who are caring for me could die before I do, and the world would still go trundling on.

To perfect — *perficere* — means to carry something all the way through. God will perfect what I leave imperfect. Complete — *complere* — means to fill up. God will fill what I have left half-empty. "And I am sure of this," Paul writes, "that he who began a good work in you will bring it to completion at the day of Jesus Christ." That is a truth to rest in today, thanks be to God.

God, whose power is made perfect in weakness, meet me today in my own weakness. Carry through to completion all the acts and intentions that I leave unaccomplished. Transform my efforts and turn them to your divine purposes. I pray this in the name of Jesus, who makes all things new. Amen.

If worldly pressures fray the mind
And love itself cannot unwind
Its tangled skein of care:
Our inward life repair.

Forgiving

. . . as the Lord has forgiven you, so you also must forgive.

COLOSSIANS 3:13

"Forgive our trespasses, as we forgive those who trespass against us." Every week for years I have spoken those words in prayer. They prod my conscience. I know I need more forgiveness from God than I've managed to extend to others. I believe that I will be forgiven because God's mercy and love extend far beyond my imagining. Still, I need to forgive, as deliberately and fully as I can.

These days I don't have much energy for long, painful conversations about past conflicts. I'm not at all sure I'm up to the visits it would take to forgive those I need to forgive in person, or to work through old hurts to the point of giving and receiving forgiveness. A few of the people I need to forgive have died. So I need to accept the mysterious fact that forgiveness is work I can do with or without their being here to receive it.

How do I do this? I can begin by remembering that forgiving them in my heart and before God releases *me* from resentments and hurt and anger that I carry like fetters. I can let go of all need to prove wrongdoing, defend my point of view, insist on my rights. I can let go of all that chains me to past unhappiness. I can accept God's own permission to dwell in the present.

I can name each of them, hold each of them up before God, and ask that whatever suffering they carry may be relieved, especially any suffering I may have caused.

I can imagine their stories from their point of view, even if that perspective has seemed wrong and self-serving to me. I can practice empathy as I remember them, asking that I be enabled to see them as brothers and sisters and love them "as myself." I can pray for the grace of compassion.

In light of death, all the matters in this life take on a different weight and meaning. I can afford, now, to take a wider view of all the hurts, misunderstandings, abuses, negligence, and inflicted pain, and see how they are entangled with need and fear and loss, and how only God can cut through those thickets to where, in me and in others, the heart of a child still beats.

Loving God, grant me forgiveness, and the grace to forgive. I lay all my resentments and old hurts and misunderstandings before you and ask you to clear my mind and heart of all that keeps me from living in love. Amen.

For the love of God is broader than the measures
    of the mind,
And the heart of the Eternal is most
    wonderfully kind. . . .

Blessings

The cup of blessing that we bless, is it not a participation in the blood of Christ?

1 CORINTHIANS 10:16

There's a story about a rabbi who responded to good news with "How do you know it's not a disaster?" and to bad news with "How do you know it's not a blessing?" It serves as a reminder that we're never in possession of all the facts, capable of imagining all the implications, or privy to God's view of our lives. I imagine all of us can look back and recognize how much grace and goodness have emerged from what seemed disasters at the time — losses, separations, failures, mistakes, all the ways we've wasted time and life that might have been better spent. Even death, even death when I'm not ready for it, even death that will leave those who depend on me bereft and sad, may have a dimension of blessing I cannot see.

I'm not ready to accept the glib notion that the loss of this life and all I love in it is a "blessing in disguise." I don't feel ready to go. Still, I can imagine that if this is to be the time and the way I go, God has a good in mind that's beyond my reckoning. It may be that when I am released from this dimension and welcomed into another, there will be blessing of a kind only hinted at in Gospel sayings about the kingdom of heaven and in the many "near death" stories of people who have been clinically "dead" and have returned to life. Those stories generally converge on experiences of unconditional love, warmth, welcome, forgiveness, and well-being. In some, the dying person can see the grief of those left behind, but knows at the same time, with deep conviction, that they'll be okay.

Without being able to say how it may be true, I can imagine that their sorrow could be turned to blessing — perhaps a deepening of faith, of gratitude, of compassion for others' suffering, of self-knowledge, of a more complex happiness. The word "blessed" has been translated "happy" in the Beatitudes. If it's true that they who mourn are blessed, it must be that mourning itself opens a space for happiness of a new kind that can only come from God. This is a time to claim that blessing — for those I leave, and for me as I go.

God, source of all blessing, bless us now as we face this parting. May my death be an occasion for your sufficient grace to be made manifest to each person who suffers from my absence. I count on the great abundance of your mercy. Amen.

Come, thou Fount of every blessing,
Tune my heart to sing Thy grace. . . .

Preparations

. . . if only I may finish my course. . . .

ACTS 20:24

"It's time to get your affairs in order." This timeworn advice to the dying seems like good common sense, but it's not altogether clear to me what it means. I've taken care of some of the obvious things — a will, an advance health care directive, assigning power of attorney, letting the people I love know my preferences about care that I may need, and about the memorial. I've told them that I love them. I've asked their forgiveness and offered them mine. I've told stories about my life to the listeners to whom my life matters.

Setting my affairs in order may simply be a matter of laying them all before Christ, who is the "finisher" of our faith. God and my family can bring to completion all that needs to be completed — all my dropped stitches, all my scattered papers, all my unreturned e-mails, all the conversations I postponed. Somehow, whatever good I hoped would come of my efforts will come in God's way and in due time. To set my affairs in order may simply be to lay those burdens down in complete trust, relying on the One who "doeth all things well."

The most important preparing is inner work now. As I pray for acceptance, pray to be set free from anxiety and fear, I also find myself thinking of what I have been taught and believe about release from this body and this life into a new one. It is a shedding that will happen in spite of me. But to enter into it with intention, awareness, and even curiosity seems an important way of making ready. I don't know what it will mean to "be ready." I don't suppose any of us is ready to meet God, though I have known some who have gone not only peacefully but joyfully after long lives formed and matured in faith. I'd like to be one of those, reaching out with open hands and heart toward whatever heavenly beings are sent to greet me and lead me home.

So even at this eleventh hour I find myself asking, like the slow-learning disciples, "Lord, teach me to pray." I think back on the many times I've prayed in preparation for challenges, losses, transitions — babies arriving, parents' new needs, job changes. I've pondered Paul's daring claim that "we have the mind of Christ" (1 Cor. 2:16) and Peter's admonition to set our minds fully "on the grace that will be brought to you at the revelation of Jesus Christ" (1 Peter 1:13). Now, especially, I want to lay aside every weight and love God with my whole mind, releasing all fear and fostering hope in wholly new ways.

It helps me to think of these days I live out as a season of preparation, and to enter them remembering that even in this life we never know exactly what we're being prepared for.

More than preparing myself, I pray to be prepared for what is to come — the letting go, the crossing, the entering — and for deep peace in the process.

Creator God, all things come from and return to you. I offer you all the tag-ends of my messy life and ask you to complete what needs completing and continue what needs to be continued. Relieve me of all anxiety about what has been "mine" to do in this life. I offer you back all that I have and all that I am. Amen.

Master, speak! And make me ready
When Thy voice is truly heard. . . .

Domestic Disagreements

Let the peace of Christ rule in your hearts. . . .

COLOSSIANS 3:15

It's unlikely that any major life event happens without awakening antagonisms. In even the most harmonious families the claims of siblings or children or spouses or parents clash at certain points. But I *belong* to them; I am a member of this family, this little organ of the body of Christ, the way my hand or my eye belongs to me, and so they have a right to lay claim to me, and to try to protect me in their various ways as death threatens to take me away.

This is a time to review all I know about boundaries. If there's conflict about how best to help me, the best I can do is be clear about what help I need, what I want, what I hope for, and then ask that they discuss their differences where I don't have to absorb the tensions.

So much comes up in a time of loss. New grief triggers old griefs, and even those who most want to bring me peace and comfort drag with them into my sickroom their painful memories of other losses, and find that renewed pain erupts into bitterness or quarrelsome feelings that take them, and me, by surprise. Often these behaviors degenerate into petty differences that might be laughable — if anyone managed to get enough distance on them to laugh.

Perhaps I can be that person. Perhaps I can be the peacemaker when people disagree about how and when to prepare meals, how much noise is acceptable, who controls incoming calls, which out-of-town folk stay where, which doctor to believe, even what movie to watch when everyone in the house is tired and frayed at the end of the day.

This is a time to pray for peace in every heart. Every heart in the circle around me is breaking in some way. Every heart is full and overflowing — and sometimes the overflow gets messy. Peace, as W. B. Yeats puts it, "comes dropping slow." Small acts of peacemaking help — open hands, a quiet smile, soothing music, even a sign outside my door, perhaps, that instead of saying "Do Not Disturb" might be more invitational: "Come into quiet, all who enter here" or "May this room be a place of peace."

Prince of Peace, bring us peace in a troubling time. Quiet our turbulent minds and open our hearts to one another, that we may be united and blessed even in our sorrow. Amen.

Wrap now Thy peace, like a mantle, around us, Guarding our thoughts and our passions controlling. . . .

The Offices of Friendship

I went about as though I grieved for my friend or my brother. . . .

PSALM 35:14

"If there's anything at all I can do, let me know." How often I've heard my friends make this offer. But, as my energy dwindles and my caregiving is increasingly overseen by a team of medical people and family folk, it's easiest for me to respond, "Thank you — there's really nothing."

But there are things they can do, and it's a kindness to them to let them participate in what's happening to me. They love me. They want to help in some way. So here's a to-do list for the dear people who want to do something. I'd like them to do this:

Pray with me and for me and, when I'm too weak to pray,
    pray on my behalf and in my stead.
Bring soup and salad and comfort to those I am leaving.
Offer your skills — be an ad-hoc accountant
    or event planner or cook or secretary.

63

Be a quiet presence when I need company
without conversation.
Protect me from needy do-gooders.
Help me laugh. Watch comedies with me. Manage
the remote.
Comfort each other so I don't have to be a dispenser
of comfort.
Spread whatever news other people need to know.
Read me Psalms and poems and passages from books
I've loved.
Be my advocate when Nurse Ratched comes on duty.
Attend to my garden.
Burn the letters I ask you to without reading them.
Listen to my dreams.
Keep listening when I'm not making sense.
Let me speak my pain.
Reassure me without trying to cheer me up.
Pray some more — with me, and for me, and in my stead.

*Jesus, friend of the poor and the suffering, be a friend to
me and to my friends in this challenging time. Let this
circle of friendship be a sacred space, filled with generosity
and imagination and hope and compassion and kindness.
Let us love one another as you have loved us. In your precious name we pray, Amen.*

*Blest be the tie that binds our hearts in Christian love;
The fellowship of kindred minds is like to that above.*

Uncomfortable Comfort

. . . who will console you? . . . who will comfort you?

I'm realizing that neither giving nor receiving comfort is simple. Some days people's efforts to comfort me make me feel loved, cared for, and less afraid. Other days they irritate me unreasonably: I don't want my pillow plumped or my hand held or news from the book club or even the flowers whose mild scent gives me little waves of nausea. I don't always want visitors, but I don't want to hurt the feelings of those whose visits are well-intended, if ill-timed. And even the visitors I do want don't always manage to leave me feeling more peaceful or grateful or kindly. I don't want illness to make me irritable, but it does.

Some days even the Scripture passages that have been mainstays for me in times of trouble, words of life that have sustained me, fail to release me from the anxiety or restlessness or boredom or resentment or rage that comes like a demon who lurks in the night.

"Give it to God," my mother used to say, and so I do. God

65

must be getting a little tired of my little "gifts" of squalid and unsorted emotion. But I have to believe that even that turning toward God in the dark, reaching out for a hand I barely believe is there, connects me with the One who sustains me in these hard and tedious days. And human hands do help.

I can teach those who approach my bedside what I need. I can trust that they will welcome that instruction. I can tell them the words I need to hear again and again, the times when touch is most important. I can tell them that solitude is sometimes a solace, that not every burst of anxiety is a crisis, that little things like leaving the door cracked open when I'm resting are important to my peace of mind. I can name my needs, humbly and specifically, and learn to receive comfort as they learn to give it.

And I can pray — single words, single phrases, single sentences that take shape on one weak breath and center me. I can travel the labyrinth past inner and outer distractions to the place where Christ awaits me, and where rest is possible once again.

Beloved Comforter, calm my fears and quiet my restless heart. Be present to me when pain comes. Teach me patience and gratitude for others' efforts. Help me also to comfort them as they face my going. Teach us trust in the time we have together, and prepare our hearts for the parting that is coming. Amen.

When other helpers fail and comforts flee,
Help of the helpless, O abide with me.

Food

My appetite refuses to touch them;
they are as food that is loathsome to me.

JOB 6:7

"You should eat a little something," I hear often these days. But I'm not hungry. That seems an especially hard fact for my sweet caregivers to accept — especially the women. Feeding is so elementally life-giving, and I'm sure that watching someone waste away while refusing food runs deeply against the grain. Still, I know that my body is getting ready to stop its work and release me into a new, subtler order of being. I have no desire for food, and very little for drink. I sometimes make the effort for those who come with what used to be my favorites — mac and cheese, fresh raspberries, hot oatmeal with cinnamon — but food turns to cardboard in my mouth, and eating is a chore.

I need them to accept what I have accepted — that sustaining my body at this point isn't the real point, and that the body has its own wisdom, which I am trying to heed. I myself need to respect what I'm learning about this process as I go through it, and pay attention to the messages of a changing body.

This body has been faithful for all these years. Even when I have abused it with excesses, looked at it with dissatisfaction and judgment, ignored its steady stream of useful information, it has allowed me a good life, and a joyful one.

But now there is to be an end to eating and drinking, digesting, dispersing hormones, and making protein. There is to be an end of movement and a time of growing still, and I am entering that time. One by one, the processes that have to stop will stop. Welcomed or not, the stages of dying will proceed.

What I want now is to go with grace across each remaining threshold. The time for "fighting" is over. I want to bid my body a grateful and gracious farewell, in faith that its purposes have been served and that the "resurrection of the body" I have proclaimed every time we rise to recite the creed will bring its own unimaginable delights.

Now, as I watch and wait, I am aware of being in a new time between the times; old things have already passed away — the birthday dinners and leisurely weekend breakfasts and midnight snacks with old movies — and all things are being made new.

As my physical appetite wanes, I pray for the grace of a sharpened appetite for God's final gifts, for rest, for assurance, for love, and for the blessing in the ordinary, inconspicuous ways those gifts come.

Bless me now, Lord, as I begin to fast while others eat the food you have provided. Thank you for the many meals I have shared, and the love around those tables. Deepen my hunger for the spiritual food of your Word and Sacrament as I prepare for your heavenly banquet. Amen.

> *Feed on His faithfulness, my soul,*
> *Who chose thee for His own. . . .*

Stuff

*Have no concern for your goods, for the best of all the
land of Egypt is yours.*

GENESIS 45:20

I think about the things I'm leaving behind. I worry sometimes about what might be unearthed and misunderstood
in my backlog of e-mails, or my journal entries written in
confusion or anger, or my receipts for things I indulged in ir-
responsibly. I wonder what might give offense, or disappoint,
or be taken out of context. I sometimes imagine a bonfire that
would destroy it all and leave only what memories provide.

But I don't have the energy now to clean up the scattering
of human messes I leave behind. I have to trust that those who
have loved me will treat my detritus and my story with loving
kindness, respect my secrecies, even if some were unwise, and
let go of what remains that testifies to silliness, selfishness,
poor judgment, or unfulfilled longings.

I can't control what becomes of all I leave behind. Though
I've made a will and expressed my wishes, there will be days
when one family member or another will haul out a box or

fish in a pocket or open a drawer and find something that will make them feel puzzled — or, worse, dismayed. Perhaps they'll come across something that they'll toss uneasily into the trash, suffering one more wave of sadness — perhaps even of resentment.

Whatever legacy I leave will be a mixed bag for others to carry. May God help them in that task, as they revisit their memories and rearrange them. I hope those memories are good ones that help them along their own journeys, but I can't insure that, any more than I've been able to insure that those I most care for are always content. This is another place to count on God's grace — that in its aftermath my life will be a source of blessing, and not a burden, to those who have shared it, and that my unsorted stuff will do no harm, but will be winnowed with care as the chaff blows away.

God of Abraham, Isaac, and Jacob, God of history, you have spoken to us through stories and called us into a shared life that stories sustain. Bless those who imagine and tell my story after I die. May the stories they keep help them on their way. Thank you for the life I have lived and for the forgiveness you have promised for all I have done or left undone to others' harm. In my death, O Lord, let me leave a blessing behind. Amen.

Let goods and kindred go, this mortal life also. . . .

Lingering

Be gracious to me, O LORD, for I am languishing. . . .

"I'm ready to go." I've heard other people say this when they were close to death — and now it's on my lips. I'm tired. Those who care for me are tired. Even these days have bright and kindly moments, small pleasures, brief shared laughter. But sometimes it hardly seems enough to keep living for. Food is unappealing, TV trivial, words wearying, news of the wider world remote, and prayer full of effort. All I want some days is to walk down that passage from this life to the next, find my way into the arms of Jesus, and rest there.

"God isn't ready to take you yet," someone said the other day. And someone else commented, "There must still be things God wants you here for." On one level, I can accept the mystery of God's purposes. On another, the lingering of my dwindling life simply seems a physiological design flaw. Dying "naturally" takes more time than I want to give it.

The birth analogy helps. Labor takes the time it takes. Some babies are born in 45 minutes; some take 48 hours. Not even obstetricians know why. The labor I'm in now feels like a holding pattern, but I know, as surely as I knew when I gave birth, or witnessed it, that new life waits at the end of this pain. "Suffering produces endurance," Paul writes, "and endurance produces character, and character produces hope." It seems a little late to be building character, and yet I realize that even now something may be taking place in me that only God, and perhaps my guardian angel, can know.

Like the people who linger in comas for weeks, my life is a mystery to me at the moment. But as I continue on this slow way, I remember the Psalmist's exuberant cry: "Let everything that has life and breath praise the LORD!" And I think that perhaps this is a good prayer for now — that each remaining breath be a quiet act of praise, that breathing itself be an offering of acceptance, that this failing body be a vessel of the great Spirit that blows where it will and fills even the faintest lungs with the air of heaven.

Lord of all slow things, of snails and sunsets and unhurried seasons, of all that grows invisibly under the topsoil and of all that ages and dies, help me endure my going hence even as my coming hither. Make me ripe for your kingdom and ready when you call. Amen.

Our times are in Thy hand;
O God, we wish them there;
Our lives, our souls, our all, we leave
Entirely to Thy care.

More Pain

I become afraid of all my suffering. . . .

This is the hard part. I've often said that I'm not particularly afraid of death, but I am afraid of pain. And here it is — the pain I can't fully assuage, which ranges from a dull ache to piercing, burning, nearly unbearable streaks of something alien racing through my body. I need all the wisdom I've gleaned from others' experience about how to handle pain. What to do with it?

Breathe. Paying attention to breath is a basic training of meditation and preparation for labor — panting when the pain is acute, then taking long, slow breaths when I'm able to relax into it, or "ride on top of the wave," or step outside it. I can't control my nervous system, but I can control my breath, and it's a powerful tool. Breath links me to the Spirit of God. God breathed into the dust we are made of. Jesus breathed on the disciples when he commissioned them to do his work. Every breath I receive and release connects me to the source of all life.

Pray. When I'm in the midst of pain, short, repetitive prayers help: "Jesus, be with me." "Hold me." "See me through."

"Come, Lord Jesus." Beads or a cross or something to hold can anchor me. A voice — even a recorded voice — of someone praying with me and for me when I can't speak my prayers can help keep me focused on the God of compassion who suffers with us and in us and for us.

Listen to music. Music can take me into and keep me in a place of prayer. Sacred music — chant, hymns, Bach chorales, praise songs — lets me enter into prayers I can't form or utter, and lifts me into a trust I can't summon on my own. Nearby I have a list of the pieces that help me, and headphones and speakers. These have become important equipment for this hard part of my journey.

Let myself be held. Or touched. I need people now who know when and how to touch me, when the simple pressure of a loving hand will diffuse or dispel the pain, when a hand holding mine offers important reassurance, when I need to be encircled and held like a child. Only certain ones bring that gift of touch. I need to ordain them to that task.

Sleep when I can. I welcome aids to sleep, and I accept the help available. Sleep, when I can have it, is a place of refuge and restoration, and I receive it with gratitude.

Loving God, you know our suffering. Be with me in mine. If it be possible, let this cup pass from me. If not, help me bear it in my body with complete trust that it will end and that you are with me in this dark valley. Amen.

O Lord, make haste to hear my cry.
To You I call, on You I rely. . . .

75

Other People's Fear

Stay with me; do not be afraid....

"I can't bear to see you in pain." When those nearest me say this, I know they're trying to express a love that longs for me to stop suffering. Still, I need them to bear it.

Some of the people I had thought would be most ready with help and presence have backed away. They call, they send things, sometimes they come, but they stay very briefly and seem uncomfortable. The frustration of not being able to relieve my suffering may be what puts distance between us, or the anxiety my dying triggers by making visible the fate that awaits us all. The fact that I am dying inevitably brings up the fact that they will, too.

Much of what passes between me and friends or family these days touches on ultimate things. The smallest acts of kindness, lapses into sadness, expressions of need, flashes of irritation, mumbled prayers — all loom large here at the edge of life and death. To be with me is to have to go to that edge, I realize, and some people aren't ready to do that. It's hard to keep things "ordinary." Ordinary feels safe. Not knowing when I might take a turn for the worse, not knowing when final good-byes will need to be said, is scary for them and for me.

Some days, though, I feel as if I've made my peace with what is coming, and they haven't. On those days it seems that I'm the one called to pray for them — that they're the people in need and I'm in an oddly privileged position. Even to say that seems a little absurd, since dying hardly feels like a privilege, but as I shed earthly hopes and ambitions and attachments to things and habits, I sometimes feel a kind of freedom from care that lightens me, and I see what burdens they carry who don't yet have this release.

What we all need now is patience and courage, in ways we may not have needed them, or understood them, before.

Giver of all good gifts, give us all the patience and the courage to see one another through. Grant us compassion in the face of each other's suffering and fear, remembering that you suffered for us and enter into all our sorrows more intimately than we imagine. Amen.

Take courage, my soul, and let us journey on,
For though the night is dark, it won't be very long. . . .

A Time to Weep

My tears have been my food day and night. . . .

People speak of "the gift of tears," and now I begin to understand that phrase more fully. I don't like to cry. I tend to weep in private, and to avoid crying when I'm with others, even those who know me best. But perhaps "there is a time to weep" is part of what I need to learn now.

Tears release me into honest sorrow. They release me from the strenuous business of finding words. They release me into a childlike place where I need to be held and can find comfort in embrace — in the arms of others and in the arms of God. Tears release me from the treadmill of anxious thoughts, and even from fear. They release me from the strain of holding them back.

Tears are a consent to what is. They wash away, at least for a time, denial and resistance. They allow me to relinquish the self-deceptive notion that I'm in control. Tears dilute resentments and wash away the flotsam left by waves of anger. Tears require that I stretch my trust and be vulnerable to those who witness and weep with me.

"Weeping may endure for a night, but joy cometh in the morning," the Psalmist says. It is a word of comfort, but I think I have hastened to the second clause a little too quickly in the past. Now I know that the night of weeping is an important part of the truth of that sentence, and one to be taken into full account. A whole night of weeping is a lot. Long, wakeful hours filled with tears sometimes seem immeasurable, sometimes intolerable. Other times the weeping comes as its own kind of consolation — a gift of tears.

I want to learn to accept that gift, the cleansing, the release, the sharing of sorrow, the opening of the heart it brings, and rest in the One who wept with us, who weeps with us, but who also promised that finally every tear will be wiped away.

Receive my tears, Jesus, when they come, and let them join with the great river of your own sorrow for a world in pain. I thank you for the gift of tears, as I also thank you for the joy that does come, still, even with the breaking light of every earthly morning I am given. Amen.

> *Gently, Lord, O gently lead us,*
> *Pilgrims in this vale of tears,*
> *Through the trials yet decreed us,*
> *Till our last great change appears. . . .*

Living the Paradox

For to me, to live is Christ and to die is gain.

PHILIPPIANS 1:21

Some days I feel acutely, voraciously alive. I believe there is life after death, and that some things in life are "little deaths," but this paradox runs deeper than that. It's almost as if there's new life in dying. I feel more sensitive to the small pleasures around me — birdsong, the way light falls on the objects in my room, the softness of the pillow when I'm near sleep. The voices I love in the next room sometimes sound like music. In some quiet moments I sense the presence of an angelic being, and I feel as though my awareness is moving further out on a spectrum that's been very narrow up till now.

Another kind of paradox is one that's harder to talk about, especially with people who will suffer from loss when I go. I'm losing them, too; I'm losing everything I've known here. But there are moments when I can actually imagine that loss — that shedding of earthly things, and even of all earthly ties — as liberation. The image of a butterfly emerging from its chrysalis may be so common as to be a cliché, but it is apt.

In the best, most surprising moments, I feel myself moving toward — rather than away from — life, and am almost exuberant at the prospect.

As I find my way, I think of the challenging definition of faith in the book of Hebrews: "the assurance of things hoped for, the conviction of things not seen." Those phrases stay with me some mornings like an audible heartbeat, enabling and sustaining me and teaching me how to make my farewells in love and faith.

Another paradox: this is the hardest thing I've ever had to do, and somehow the easiest. I'm so weak that I have to live in almost complete dependence and trust. At its best, it's the kind of "freefall" Denise Levertov speaks about in her beautiful poem "The Avowal," where the speaker's longing and prayer is to "attain" that effortless self-abandonment into "all-surrounding grace." On the best days I know that all-surrounding grace, and the freedom it brings, and the hope, and the peace. There is life in this dying, and I want to have it abundantly.

Lord, help me to live into the paradoxes with curiosity and willingness. Teach me again that every "no" is surrounded by a much bigger "yes." Help me to embrace the life I have now — each day of it — knowing it will end, trusting that there is life to come. Amen.

Yea, when this flesh and heart shall fail,
And mortal life shall cease,
I shall possess, within the veil,
A life of joy and peace.

Unlikely Laughter

At destruction and famine you shall laugh,
and shall not fear the beasts of the earth.

JOB 5:22

Sometimes I'm surprised by laughter. It seems one of the surest signs of hope. It comes like a fresh breeze, unanticipated, in unlikely moments. It's hard to share my laughter with people who are grieving with me and for me, but there's a certain freedom in knowing I'm not going to get better that gives me a different distance on the small stuff. Even my own infirmities sometimes slip from the tragic into the comic for a few moments. The clumsiness of cups with straws, slipping pillows, losing my phone under a strange topography of blankets, the social awkwardness and misfired remarks of dutiful visitors — all these small moments offer comic relief. And they *are* a relief. I thank God for those I can laugh with.

Laughter takes me into a larger place. J. R. R. Tolkien uses the term "eucatastrophe" to describe the happy opposite of catastrophe promised in Scripture: that all shall be well, that the heavenly banquet is the final scene, that the human adventure is comedy in its widest sense, and that all our yesterdays have actually lighted fools the way to a kingdom that comes and is already among us. In Christopher Fry's wonderful play *The Lady's Not for Burning*, a character who is struggling with thoughts of death bursts out, "For God's sake, shall we laugh . . . since laughter is surely/the surest touch of genius in creation." It is, he later observes, "an ir-relevancy/which almost amounts to revelation." "For God's sake" is a good reason to claim the gift of laughter at a time like this.

And so there are moments when I feel I can afford to laugh. It may not be "the best medicine" — not medicine as lasting and healing as prayer or intimate, enlivening conversation — but it certainly offers a salve to the day's particular hurts. One of the best comedians I know, the writer Anne Lamott, takes on very dark material: addiction, a parent's brain cancer, war, poverty, domestic struggles. But she invites us to laugh in the face of our demons and in the midst of all the ills that flesh is heir to. And like Lear's fool, she shows us how to be playful in the midst of the storm.

That kind of playfulness seems to me to model trust in a practical, usable way. So I keep two of Lamott's books, *Traveling Mercies* and *Plan B*, nearby to dip into when I'm down. They're not the Gospel of John or the prayers of St. Francis, but they are spiritual nourishment nonetheless, and they lighten the heavy hours of dusk and day's end.

God of light and life, I thank you for laughter. Let it be holy laughter that loosens the grip of anxiety and fear and pain and restores my hope in all you have promised us at the end of this bumpy and unpredictable journey. Amen.

Dance, then, wherever you may be.
I am the Lord of the Dance, said he. . . .

Memories

And you shall remember the whole way that the Lord
your God has led you these forty years. . . .

DEUTERONOMY 8:2

Among other kindly services, hospice offers help with what
they call "life review." Someone comes to record whatever
memories you want to collect for the benefit of those you're
leaving behind. Recording my memories brings up an interesting question that historians have raised about the "uses of
the past."

I can think of several purposes that a life review might
serve: the enjoyment of children and grandchildren and old
friends who might even find new bits of insight in my stories; a record of a point of view that might jar a few people
into examining their own; a voice from a generation that will
help another generation take some measure of their own assumptions; a way of challenging my siblings' notions about
our family; an offering to my spouse; a kind of "spiritual
autobiography". . . .

It might serve purposes I don't even imagine. One that bears considering is the pleasure it gives me simply to remember. I can trawl through a huge inventory of mental snapshots — some of them unlabeled and puzzling, some of them vivid as the rose that just opened this morning. I can remember sensations that still quicken my heart or find a place in my body — straddling my mother's hip as she held me and swayed and sang; feeding ducks in the park; quarreling with my brother over Monopoly; the smell of the pepper tree in the schoolyard; pulling out my own tooth; memorizing Bible verses with Miss Ruby in Sunday school; feeling the first nudgings of doubt when I thought about Shadrach, Meshach, and Abednego; the pain of an infected cut on my knee; the pleasures of rereading *Winnie-the-Pooh* with my grandmother; the fear I felt when I first really listened to the ten o'clock news; feeling awkward at school dances; the full-hearted thrill of first love in my senior year; discovering real delight in reading Steinbeck, and then Shakespeare; feeling empowered when I "got" photosynthesis; the pain of breaking up; the unsettling encounter with a homeless person who taught me to look again. Once I pull on the thread, memories keep coming. I see even the small ones in new terms now, as learning moments, colorful chips in a kaleidoscope that keeps producing new designs, shards of something once whole that offer new possibilities.

Some memories are painful but valuable, and worth telling. I record them in hope that others can be spared similar pain, or learn from them. I don't want my children to suffer from marital misunderstandings, or financial failure from imprudent risks, or the fear that keeps them from taking worthwhile risks.

Some of the memories seem like messages to particular individuals. I want my son to know how I cherished the task of seeing him through a long illness. I want my spouse to know I haven't forgotten the small rituals that grounded me in the morning, or the sound of his voice reading the Psalms. I want my niece to know how I remember her mother and grandmother. Thinking of my own memories as parting gifts gives me energy to share them.

I remember a pastor friend asking, as he pondered new situations, "I wonder what God's up to here?" Seeing my life moments as a record of what God has been "up to" shores me up as I come to my conclusions. The record I leave may bear witness to divine mystery in ways I can't now fathom for those who care to read it. May it serve purposes beyond my own.

Gracious God, you gave us the gift of memory. Bless what remains in mine as I offer it to those I love. Bless their remembering and their forgetting; may both be manifestations of your loving-kindness toward us in our brokenness. As we see this story we have lived, remind us of the larger story we inhabit. Amen.

> *Praise Him, still the same forever,*
> *Slow to chide and swift to bless. . . .*

The Bad Days

For my sighing comes instead of my bread,
and my groanings are poured out like water.

JOB 3:24

Some days it's too much. The pain, the tedium, the bleak-
ness and blankness are unbearable. I feel myself sinking into
murky waters of depression, irritability, restlessness, and anxiety. I don't even have the energy that pure anger provides,
or the will to pray my way out of this. My feelings aren't just
mixed — they're hopelessly tangled. I don't want to see even
the people who care about me most, but I don't want them to
go away, either. I'd give anything to escape my boredom, but
no entertainment seems enticing.

It didn't take Job long to launch into lament: already in
the third chapter he spends 26 verses wondering why he
was born at all and, having suffered that misfortune, why
he keeps on living when he'd so much rather die. To readers
who suffer, Job offers permission to rant. It takes a long time
to get to the happy ending, and though Job is faithful, he's
not cheerful. He doesn't pretend. He doesn't look on the

bright side. His misery isn't a parable he's pondering — it's misery.

The Psalmist didn't pretend, either. He gave himself a lot of room to object when he felt abandoned, desperate, victimized, or otherwise undone. Over a quarter of the Psalms are psalms of individual lament. "O LORD, how many are my foes!" he writes. "Consider my groaning." "See my affliction." "How long will you hide your face from me?" Eventually he comes around to reaffirmation and praise, but not until he's registered some lengthy and bitter complaints.

Jesus' cry from the cross — "My God, my God, why have you abandoned me?" — sanctifies lament as a dimension of prayer. His visceral truth-telling surely makes room for our cries.

I remember reading with some satisfaction Barbara Ehrenreich's edgy book, *Bright-Sided,* where she points out the dangers and fallacies of "positive thinking." Occasionally a visitor comes who's a little too determined to cheer me up, and I do feel "bright-sided" — bullied by the pressure to put praise and gratitude before lament. On days like today I need to claim all the shadowy space that Scripture opens up for exploring the darkness.

The only visitors I want are the ones who can let me — and even help me — do that. My theology right now has to include room for some unconsoling truth. I need my 26 verses. Maybe then I can find my way back to reassurance and rest and thanksgiving. Maybe then I can close my eyes on the final lines of one of the Psalmist's complaints: "In peace I will both lie down and sleep; for you alone, O LORD, make me dwell in safety."

God of all consolation, come to me in my darkest hours.
I no longer know what to hope for or how to hope. Meet
me here at the edge of Sheol and hold me with your right
hand. Let me lie down in peace and sleep in safety. Amen.

Be still, my soul: though dearest friends depart
And all is darkened in the vale of tears;
Then shalt thou better know His love, His heart,
Who comes to soothe thy sorrows and thy fears.

Looking Ahead

"Surely I am coming soon." Amen. *Come, Lord Jesus!*
REVELATION 22:20

"When a man gets to be 80," Malcolm Cowley wrote, "it's time to look ahead." My inclination to look back is strong. On my darker days it's tempting to look back in regret. On my better days I look back in gratitude. But looking back at all may be a diversion from the more important matter of looking ahead.

It's hard for me to know how to think about "heaven" — it's such a contaminated idea. I let go of pastel images that involved clouds and harps a long time ago. The family reunion in the sky also seems too simple, though I do find myself hoping to see people I've loved again. The image of the twelve-gated city in the book of Revelation is dazzling, but remote. Jesus' "Kingdom of Heaven" statements — it's within you, among you, like a mustard seed, like a woman who has lost a coin — are helpful, but mysterious. Stories of near-death experiences are fascinating and give me a more palpable sense that I'm about to embark on a wild, adventurous journey into the next dimension.

The notion of heaven I keep coming back to is simply

home. I'm going home. I believe, from all I've read and heard and imagined, that I will be met, accompanied, welcomed, forgiven, completely accepted, and unconditionally loved. I believe that death will be similar to birth — going through a dark and difficult passage into amazing light and new life.

It helps to remember that every single human being has gone or will go through this, and that both Scripture and a huge body of testimony provide good reason for confidence that we go on from here to a liberating new life. I have days when I'm afraid of death, days when I'm fairly free of anxiety about it, and days when I feel a curious exhilaration, knowing I'm being prepared for encounter with the One who has met me in the Eucharist, and in the silence of prayer, and in many moments of sweet surprise.

Jesus says, "I go to prepare a place for you." His words suggest that what we can expect when we die is divine hospitality — loving welcome to a place we'll know unconditional love and belonging. There is deep comfort in both these things — that every single person on earth will have a turn to do this, and that we're not going into "vacant interstellar spaces," but into a loving place where we're "no more a stranger, nor a guest, but like a child at home."

God of amazing grace, lead me home. Take away my fear of dying, and let me lie down in peace and sleep, "for you alone, O Lord, make me dwell in safety." Amen.

With open face and joyful heart,
We then shall see Thee as Thou art. . . .

What Am I Waiting For?

My soul also is greatly troubled.
But you, O LORD — how long?

PSALM 6:3

Though I know those who love me are praying that my death might be postponed a little longer, I have days when I feel quite ready. As the hymn says, "I am tired, I am weak, I am worn." I've taken care of what I can here, and I can feel myself slipping away even from those dearest to me. I look at them and see that they'll heal; they'll find their way; the love they've directed so faithfully toward me will fuel other parts of their lives now. This parting is not the worst thing. Harder, these days, is coping with the possibility of long, painful lingering.

But then there are those days when I wake into ambivalence and confusion. I'd like to "let go," but it's not as easy as it sounds. The body is persistent, as is love of this life, which these days is sustained mostly by the faces of the people I so love. Even when I think of dying as relief and release from pain, it grieves me to think of leaving them.

Still, it's exhausting to remain in what seems like a holding pattern day after day. "Our days on earth are like a shadow," says the writer of Chronicles, "and there is no abiding." But I am abiding. "O Lord of mysteries, how baffling, how clueless/ is laggard death," Denise Levertov wrote in "Death Psalm: O Lord of Mysteries." That poem speaks the truth with appropriate irony that I face every day now: I have made ready, I have bid farewell, I have set my face toward Jerusalem, but my time has not yet come, and I don't know what might still be required to reach that "fullness of time" when my assignment here is completed and I am allowed to leave.

I don't pray to die. I don't long to die. But I am waiting to die, and not sure what the waiting is for. A final chance to practice patience, perhaps. Or complete submission. Or listening. Or maybe a chance for some soul work that I don't even need to know about, but that may be wrought in me for a good beyond my understanding. A reminder that my times are in God's hands.

Loving Creator, as you knitted me together in my mother's womb, unknit me in due time, and release me into the new life you have prepared. In the meantime, make me patient, and those around me also, welcoming each day I am given. Amen.

> *His purposes will ripen fast,*
> *Unfolding every hour. . . .*

Not Before I'm Gone

O LORD, *make me know my end,*
  and what is the measure of my days. . . .

PSALM 39:4

I know it's inevitable that other people have to make some decisions for me now, and take care of things I'd rather take care of myself. It isn't loss of authority over the big things that bothers me most of the time, but loss of authority over the small, daily matters that were once my prerogative and my pleasure to attend to. Someone else waters the plants and decides when the dog should be walked. Someone else decides when to declutter the family room and when the roses need pruning. Someone else vets my phone calls and writes out the grocery list.

Bless their hearts for doing these things. But I need them also to recognize how important it is to me to remain a full participant in family life as long as it's at all possible. I don't want the furniture rearranged, except what has to be moved for the hospital bed and the cumbersome equipment I need now. I don't want the ceremony of dinnertime to dissolve into ad-hoc snacking just because I can't come to the table. I don't want the languishing houseplants removed; I want them tended to with the patience it takes to keep them alive.

It's still my home, until I move on to a new one. I'm here in body and mind, even though both are failing. I want to be consulted as well as cared for. I want to write my own signature even when it's shaky, and to fasten my own clothing even when I'm slow. I want to stand and walk when I have the energy, even though I need support, and to be left alone when I need solitude, even though, as some of them seem to fear, I might die before they come back.

I want those who care for me to work *with* me, not just *for* me. I need not to feel displaced from this home, this place on earth that has been so precious to me, and a site of such happiness. I have felt grounded and empowered here, located and equipped for what I've needed to do. Here is where I've extended hospitality to others; I don't want to feel like a guest in my own home. Instead, I want to feel that I'm bringing my time here to a fitting closure, with whatever rituals of departure I — not others — may need to enact.

So I need to find the words to ask for that particular courtesy — that the changes others may want to make be postponed, if they can be, for the time it takes me to take my leave.

Holy One, you have located us in time and space. Help us to take each step of this journey in "due time," knowing there is a time to wait and a time to act, a time to hold

and a time to relinquish, and to remember each day that
all our times are in your hands. Amen.

Be Thou our guide while life shall last,
And our eternal home. . . .

Opportunity

This will be your opportunity to bear witness.

LUKE 21:13

The idea of a "good death" has a long history. People used to pray for one, and prepare for it. That practice has fallen largely out of favor, but it may be worth retrieving. A "good death" meant one that offered a chance to repent, confess, make amends to those one had harmed, and make one's peace with God — blessings that come with a gradual and conscious dying. I'd probably add the prayer that my dying might in some way be a gift and a witness to those around me — that I might take it as one more opportunity to refract grace into the world.

I have a chance now to reach a new level of honesty. Not that I've been generally dishonest, but dying strips away even the habit of small social deceptions that keep everyone inside the comfort zone. The penultimate line from the old wedding rite — "Let him speak now or forever hold his peace" — comes to mind as I consider what conversations need to happen, and on what terms. I have a chance to say last things. It's a little like one of those writing assignments teachers gave: If you could keep only one thing on a desert island, what would it be? If you could say one thing you haven't said to your father, what would it be? If you knew you had only six months to live, what would you do with them?

There's a reason why Professor Randy Pausch's "Last Lecture" — delivered after he was given three to six months to live with pancreatic cancer — went viral on the Internet. People want to hear from those who are dying. And facing death first-hand confers a kind of privilege: people listen. I suppose dying calls us all to listen intently, watch, and pray, to drop to a deeper level of awareness as we consider what we are about and why we were called to walk this journey.

Since I am a focal point of others' attention, I'd like to step graciously into my role — not to play household saint, but to be explicit about my concerns, about the hope that is in me, about what matters to me now, about my pain, and certainly about my love. My father died unable simply to say "I love you," though I believe he did. The chance to say it and impart it in new ways is mine now — a chance to do for Dad what he couldn't, in that mysterious way in which we fill in each other's potholes and gaps to make whole the body of Christ. It's an opportunity I don't want to miss.

God of grace, grant me the grace of a good death. Let my consent to this call be an occasion for deeper conversation, a deepening of the faith we share, and a deepening trust in you, who hold us all as we make our way through this world, setting our sails toward home. Amen.

When peace, like a river, attendeth my way,
When sorrows like sea billows roll;
Whatever my lot, Thou hast taught me to say,
"It is well, it is well with my soul."

Doubt

*Jesus immediately reached out his hand and took hold
of him, saying to him, "O you of little faith, why did you
doubt?"*

MATTHEW 14:31

I have very dark days. Late afternoons, especially, my demons
arrive: depression, emotional torpor, resentment, doubt. The
doubt disturbs me most — when all the affirmations, prayers,
words I've received in *lectio divina,* sermons, and life-giving
images recede into the shadows, and I find myself on the edge
of an abyss.

I wonder if my faith is a figment. I wonder if life really is
eternal, or if I'm heading toward oblivion. I wonder if people
who preach a bleak and terrible doctrine of hell are right. I
wonder about Buddhists, Hindus, Jews, Muslims, Zoroastrians,
shamans, agnostics — so many who haven't followed the faith
I have claimed but have brought light and wisdom into the
world. I wonder whether my theology — or the God I imagine
and pray to — is too small. These wonderings lead me away
from prayer and into anxiety. And anxiety is a lonely place.

"Praise the good angel Doubt," Mark Van Doren writes in his unsettling poem "Praise Doubt," which concludes with lines that come back to me in the darkness:

Praise him. He believes
In the long day we are given.
Praise him. He dances upon the whitecaps.

Ironically, practiced doubters seem to proceed in a strange confidence that there is room enough and time enough to explore the shadows, the psychological outback where the questions lie that leave me writhing in frustration. I've heard many times that doubt is part of the life of faith. I have to seek comfort in that, and in the stories of Peter and Thomas.

Peter's story is dire. He's out on the water, can't believe in the miracle he's seeing, and sinks. Just when he thinks he's going to drown, Jesus reaches out and takes hold of him. Even though what follows is a rebuke — "O you of little faith, why did you doubt?" — Peter is saved and safe. Some days I find myself up to my neck in the churning water with no help in sight. But in this story, and in the one where Thomas refuses to believe, Jesus reaches out his hand.

It isn't words or explanation that saves these two. It's a simple, direct, human act: Jesus gives them a hand. He takes Thomas's hand and puts it in his side. He takes Peter's hand and lifts him out of the water. I need him to take my hand when I'm word-weary and world-weary and theologically exhausted. These days of doubt are a time to claim the wonderful hymn "Precious Lord, Take My Hand." I can rest in that prayer and wait "through the storm, through the night."

Jesus, as you helped Peter and Thomas, help me now. Help my unbelief. Calm my fear. Open my eyes. Guide my hand to your side. Meet me in my weakness and carry me a while until I can walk joyfully in faith once more. Amen.

So help me in my unbelief and let my life be true. . . .

Other People's Pain

Lord, when did we see you hungry or thirsty or a
stranger or naked or sick or in prison, and did not
minister to you?

MATTHEW 25:44

Sometimes it's a bit of an annoyance to be the object of so
many people's attention. I'm so blessed to be surrounded by
those who love me. But I'm also tired of providing medical
updates in response to their queries, and of the self-focus that
comes with all this attention. I don't think it's healthy, even
in these final days or weeks, to play into a sickroom drama
that's all about me.

I've been thinking of dying as a calling. I can fully identify
now with others who are sick and dying. They are my com-
patriots. They are my companions on this last stretch. The
person in the next hospital bed, the people in the support
group, the others who are named on the prayer list — these
are my people.

Several years ago a friend who was dying of cancer went
with her husband to a workshop about death and dying. In the

course of the evening, those who were dying were sent to one room, and their partners or spouses to another. It was a stark reminder to all of them that they had separate work to do. My friend found herself bonding with other people who had cancer, exchanging stories and coping strategies. Her husband found himself oddly relieved, after initial resistance, at having to go a separate way.

We who are dying need something from each other that others can't provide. Simply being willing to seek one another out — to draw back the curtain in our semi-private hospital room, to venture out in the wheelchair on a visit, to make a call to acknowledge that we are in this together — is a ministry of presence. While I have the strength to extend that kindness to others who are dying, and receive it, I believe I'll be given access to a special kind of comfort.

Of course, in a very real sense we take those final steps alone, and no one can go with us. But in another sense, we are not alone — not for a moment. Even as we die, others are dying. Dying is what we all do, and every day millions are doing it; some of them will die the very day and hour I do. I want to hold them in my awareness and in my prayers. I want to find ways to walk with them on this journey, greet them and give them a hand when I can, or a word of encouragement, or some strategy for coping. It's what I have to offer now. I don't want to waste this chance to be generous in a whole new way.

God, you care for all your children. Many of them are dying today, this week, this month. I lift them up, asking that you surround them with your light, that you send angels to minister to them, that you come to them as Comforter, and that you gather us all to yourself as we complete our earthly journeys. Amen.

> O Jesus, blest Redeemer, sent from the heart of God,
> Hold us, who wait before Thee, near to the heart of
> God. . . .

This Body

Or do you not know that your body is a temple of the Holy Spirit . . . ?

1 CORINTHIANS 6:19

Years ago I attended an autobiography workshop in which we were given exercises to help us revisit and reframe our life stories. One exercise involved writing dialogues with our bodies, and listening for what our bodies might have to tell us. The process was revealing: my body had a lot to say — not all of it complimentary — about the ways I'd neglected it, been ashamed of it, found fault with it. It also reminded me how faithful it had been to my intentions, how resilient and how often a channel of delight.

Mary Oliver begins her exuberant poem "The Plum Trees" with a cry of pleasure over the delights that enter us on the "rivers" of our five senses. Her affirmation of the pleasure we call physical — which, like St. Thomas, she understands as the basis of the mind's knowing — offers generous permission and acceptance.

It took me a long time to come to that kind of gratitude.

Evangelicals of my parents' generation seem to have borne a heavy legacy of suspicion of the body and its pleasures. Only gradually could I lay down that burden and embrace the body I was given as a gift and an instrument of grace. Oliver showed me how to bring sensuality and spirituality together in a dance of thanksgiving.

Now my body, with all its beautiful, delicate systems, is shutting down. My organs are sluggish, my skin is dry, my hands are cold, my digestion is irregular, my immune system is depleted. I complain about these things, and sometimes resent them. But today I just want to dwell in thanksgiving for the life I have had in this body.

Every week I say with the whole congregation, "I believe in the resurrection of the body." But I also believe that doctrine is a great mystery, and that the resurrected body isn't likely to be reassembled parts that look like this one. I'm moving on into a new dimension, not back into the familiar. So I feel moved to say good-bye to this body that has done me such good service. Here is my litany of gratitude and my elegy for the body I was given.

For a safe passage from the womb into the world, I thank you, God.
For sturdy limbs that lifted me into trees and up rocky paths, I thank you, God.
For eyes and ears that opened to orchestras and ocean waves, I thank you, God.
For hands to hold babies and plant onions and write letters and open in prayer, I thank you, God.

For a tongue that let me taste cinnamon and fresh bread
and all the fruits of summer, I thank you, God.
For a heart whose beat has held me steady, I thank you,
God.
For my brain and its rich imaginings, I thank you, God.
For sleep, and rest, and respite from pain, I thank you,
God.
For all I have borne in this mortal flesh and all it has
taught me, and the way it has given shape to spirit, I
thank you, God.
May I live gratefully each remaining day of life in this
body and, when the time comes, leave it with grace.
Amen.

Let all mortal flesh keep silence. . . .

Growing as I Go

For this is the will of God, your sanctification. . . .

If a visitor were to assure me that these days of dying are an opportunity for spiritual growth, it would probably sound like a glib search for a silver lining. I might think, *Easy for you to say.* There are so many hours of lead, so much fatigue and flatness of spirit — it is hard in light of what seems like relentless loss to recognize what is being refined by this fire.

Yet when I ask myself how I have been changed in facing my own death, I realize how grace does come through suffering, and how suffering produces endurance, and endurance produces character, and character produces hope. Hope is a different thing now than in my healthier days. It's more open-ended, less focused on expectations of my own making, less about the familiar satisfactions of this life — or about this life at all.

I find that in diminished appetites for food, entertainment, photos, games, and stories, a place of inner quiet has opened up. I am taken by surprise into moments of inexplicable joy. I am occasionally aware of an abiding, witnessing presence. I find that my faith has become more childlike — not dumbed down, but also not entangled by intellectual wrestlings. I can claim in some new way the "sure and certain faith" Paul speaks about, and affirm with new clarity, "I know whom I have believed."

In my weakness is God's strength. In my weakness I am living the truth that theologians insist on: it is God who does the work of salvation and sanctification, as it is God who does the work of creation. Our part is to consent and turn toward the light as plants do. As my energies wane and even that small turning feels like effort, I imagine being met by a father who runs down the road to meet me, not waiting for my prodigal feet to complete the journey.

I love that the ancient Hebrew word for "obey" also means "listen" (sh'ma). I find myself listening. When I can't pray, I recall Mother Teresa's description of her prayer: "I listen." And I remember her acknowledgment of God's part: "He listens." I'm making new connections between listening, submission, and freedom.

A dear friend once told me of a dream in which he received this message: "The more I yield, the freer I am." These words give me direction now. I can yield, and claim what new freedom comes.

Loving God, you meet us where our energies fail and where we falter and fall. Bend my will and all my incomplete works to your holy will and make me completely willing to endure what I must in patience and hope, and to leave this life gratefully in your good time. Amen.

While we do His good will, He abides in us still,
And with all who will trust and obey. . . .

Presences

You have visited me by night. . . .

PSALM 17:3

Last night, someone was in the room with me. People are in and out all the time these days, even at nighttime, but this was different. I felt witnessed, accompanied, held, and blessed by a presence I couldn't name. I don't really need to give it a name, though I believe in angels, and in the special ways the Spirit may show up, and that Jesus is with us always and God is omnipresent. All these are matters of belief. The visitor who came last night infused those beliefs with an immediacy and an intimacy that felt both natural and mysterious.

It's hard to speak of such things, even to the people I love and trust. These days, drugs can be mind-altering and neurological signals confused. This was a sacred moment I don't want to submit to analysis or kindly condescension or clinical dismissiveness. It filled me, and fills me still, with peace and gratitude. It brought a sense of light, though not light visible to the eye, and stirred the air so subtly I would hardly call it movement, but something more like a shift in ambient energy.

I think I am being met and reassured: I won't have to travel this passage alone. I am not alone. Love bids me welcome.

Intermittently I've taken an interest in accounts of angels and apparitions. I'm not sure why they're received with such trepidation — even by believers who have every reason to recognize how natural and supernatural intersect, or perhaps blend into each other like colors in a rainbow. Helpers show up, sometimes in ordinary human garb, prevent an accident, calm a panic, or provide needed money, and then disappear without explanation. An image of Jesus rises suddenly in the mind's eye, and the room seems filled with presence. People who have had near-death experiences offer vivid descriptions of beings who meet them — sometimes familiar, sometimes not — to usher them into a new place.

I have every confidence that I am being and will be cared for by both earthly and heavenly helpers. Perhaps I have been all along. "Do not neglect to show hospitality to strangers," the author of Hebrews writes, "for thereby some have entertained angels unawares." Maybe what is unusual is not the nighttime visitation, but the fact that I'm being made newly aware of it. "Do not be afraid," angels say again and again in Scripture, and I am not. The benevolence of the visitor who came to my bedside eased me into complete trust — a place I want to dwell every moment of my remaining life.

Thank you, God, for heavenly help. Let me not miss any chance to extend hospitality to your servants, but receive them with gratitude. Amen.

Here I am, Lord. It is I, Lord.
I have heard you calling in the night. . . .

Listening

If anyone has ears to hear, let him hear.

MARK 4:23

A friend of mine who has taught music for many years asks her students to make a list of music they would want to hear if they were dying. Inspired by her, and knowing that day is coming, I have made one, though it gets emended with some regularity: Bach's "Bist du bei mir." The second movement of Schubert's Quintet in C Major. John Rutter's "Be Thou My Vision." Samuel Barber's Adagio for Strings. Celtic fiddle music.

I listen more and differently now to both music and words. Though it seems a little odd to put it this way, the pace of things hasn't changed, but I listen more slowly. What was once background takes my whole attention. What I hear holds me, somehow, as though it has possibility and importance I never noticed before. As I find food less and less appealing, I find increased nourishment in music and poetry.

Even the natural sounds outside my window seem to summon my attention in new ways. I love the sound of the mourning dove and the chittering finches in the walnut tree.

When it's quiet, I can hear the sound of the stream in the distance. That sound in particular — water tumbling over rocks — soothes me when I'm troubled, and I think of the arresting line from a poem by Wendell Berry: "The impeded stream is the one that sings." So much for me now is impeded, stopped, blocked — but the spirit finds a pathway through my ears.

Being physically slowed has opened my ears. When I'm not in pain, it seems to me I'm able to listen more deeply, both to outer and to inner voices. I've never been one to claim that God "spoke" to me, though I've often felt guided and directed. But these days the veil thins between the conversations that keep me connected to life around me and the subtler callings and moments of what I might call awakening. I feel accompanied and addressed in new ways — not dramatic, or even describable, but comforting and challenging. As other capacities fail, I feel called to listen, and to hold and be held in what I hear.

Loving God, give me ears to hear. Teach me to listen faithfully and with an open heart as I prepare to take my leave of those whose voices I have loved. Attune me to the voices that speak from heavenly places, and the call that guides me home. Amen.

I am Thine, O Lord, I have heard Thy voice. . . .

Seeing

He has made everything beautiful in its time.

ECCLESIASTES 3:11

I am aware of how many times over the past years I've walked past the paintings on my walls without noticing them. Now and then I've paused to take renewed pleasure in them, but much of the time my gaze has reverted to the bed to be made or the scattered papers to organize. Especially now that my mobility is so reduced, I remember Baby Suggs in Toni Morrison's novel *Beloved.* As she was dying in the middle of an Ohio winter, she was "hungry for color." She was hungry for orange and pink and red.

I am similarly hungry for pleasures of the eye. I see things differently now — partly bidding them good-bye, I suppose, partly just learning that slowing allows me to take in what I see, and, in a sense, to "take it personally." I'm reminded of a story about a pear tree outside the bedroom window of a woman who is terribly ill. She is often left alone, but a branch of the pear tree reaches toward her window and then into it, growing toward her as if to offer her the hand humans have not. I'm surrounded by human hands, but I see the plants in the garden and in the pots in my room as friendly presences, too. I see line and color and design in things and wonder if some artistic gift is blossoming in this eleventh hour.

I remember a friend who, when asked if she was a musician, answered yes. And when she was asked what instrument she played, she said, "None. I listen." Then, putting her hand somewhere between her solar plexus and her heart, she added, "I hear it in here." I'm beginning to see that way, addressing the creatures and objects around me and being addressed by them. "Deep calls to deep," the Psalmist writes. That line might describe a long look at a Japanese maple or an iris as well as the cosmic rumblings of the firmament.

These days I can't do much that is active. But I can and do bear witness. I see what goes on between hospice people, caregivers, and family members. I see flickers of expression that speak about suppressed pain or fatigue or distraction or hope. Witnessing is a vocation unto itself, whether or not anything is spoken. It's a way of turning seeing into prayer. "Charge me to see in all bodies the beat of spirit," Richard Wilbur wrote — a prayer that has new meaning as I look and look at familiar things until, sometimes, they become astonishing.

You who gave sight to the blind, open my eyes. Let my farewell to the sights of this world be faithful. I give you thanks for the beauty in it. I lift up the subtle sadnesses that remain in shadows. May my seeing be blessed and blessing. Amen.

Open my eyes, that I may see
Glimpses of truth Thou hast for me. . . .
Open my eyes; illumine me,
Spirit divine.

Ceremony

. . . you shall be gathered to your grave in peace. . . .

2 KINGS 22:20

I used to think I didn't care about my funeral. When the subject came up, I generally laughed and reminded people, "I won't be there. The rest of you can organize whatever helps you — sitting in a mournful circle or telling carefully edited stories about me or partying, if you like." But I'm realizing I *do* care about it to some extent. Conversations with others who have planned memorials have made me realize that the occasion will bring together people who might not otherwise come into conversation and that it may be a ministry to them in their grieving. My service can be a message of love and, God willing, an occasion of grace.

The hymns that are sung can speak for me. I have been nurtured by hymns all my life, from the time my mother sang me "Trust and Obey" as a lullaby. "Be Thou My Vision" has been a personal prayer that I might see with eyes of compassion. In the course of a day, certain phrases come back to me: "Thou my best thoughts by day or by night," "thy presence my light," "heart of my own heart." Those who know me will recognize in those words a measure of my own hope and perhaps claim the prayers a little more deeply.

The ancient hymn "Of the Father's Love Begotten," with its haunting melody, opens mysterious, cosmic space and time: "He the alpha and omega, he the source, the ending he." I would hope it would invite all who gather to see my story in a larger context, one where it mingles with all human stories, rife with learning, sorrow and delight, mistakes and forgiveness, in which God has the final word.

I imagine how Scriptures that have sustained me might offer comfort to others — Psalm 139, or the prologue to the Gospel of John, or Jesus' encounter with the woman at the well.

I can request that the focus not be on me alone, but on all who are walking the dark valley of loss, and on resurrection hope. I want the message to be unsentimental, even a little edgy. I want people to reflect on their own lives as well as on mine. And I want them to know I died in complete trust that a door would open into what Jonathan Edwards called "a world of love," where healing and welcome obliterate suffering.

I want the disposal of this body that has served me well to be done in a way that feels right to those whose bodies I have loved and held and nurtured with my own. I want them to know that I cherish the confidence uttered in Job: "Though worms destroy this body, yet in my flesh shall I see God."

I'm not much of a detail person; I would have failed miserably as an event planner. So, though I have opinions about flowers (irises and baby's breath) and fonts (Papyrus) and biblical translations (ESV) and scheduling (late afternoon, with a simple meal afterwards), I can rest easy knowing that I've added my efforts to those of my dear ones to "see me off" with dignity and grace and a little room for laughter.

Lord of Mary and of Martha, I ask your blessing on the service that follows my death. Comfort those who gather, deepen their hope in things not seen, open their hearts to forgive me and themselves whatever has not been set right among us, and give them real joy in the midst of grief, remembering how we have been gifts to each other and held in your loving care. Amen.

Some bright morning, when this life is over,
I'll fly away. . . .

Bequeathing

Which of you, if your son asks for bread, will give him a stone?

MATTHEW 7:9

I've sometimes found myself slightly amused when I've come to Jesus' assumptions that we parents know how to give good gifts to our children. We try. I've tried. I've also noticed that sometimes my children haven't been ready to receive what I've wanted to give, or have needed something I couldn't give them, or have found my bread a little overdone or stony with conditions and explanations. Of course, I'm also aware that I've given them gifts I had no idea I was giving, and that giving and receiving among us have taken place in the midst of a healthy flow of love that washes away most of the bumps in the process.

But the business of disposing of my earthly goods is tricky. As energy allows, I think it is my business to try to prevent jealousies, hurt feelings, and disappointment among those who have a claim on the things I leave behind, hoping they will share what remains without resentment.

The money is easy to distribute. Things of economic value are less complicated, I think, than things of symbolic value. I know, for instance, that I've divided monetary assets equally among my children, and there should be little to complain about. I also know that one daughter, who considers herself the family historian, wants my mother's letters. I know another would cherish my Celtic ring. My tattered copy of *Winnie-the-Pooh* may be a bone of contention — or not. Perhaps I'm wrong in thinking that the things which have sentimental value to me will hold the same resonance for them. My parents' rosewood chest may have to go to whoever has the space for it. I've asked them to name things they especially want, and I will try to honor that. Still, as my energy wanes, so does my interest in any of my possessions.

I've been pretty good at culling and pruning along the way. I've tried to model a certain detachment from most things, and have recommended Thoreau's *Walden,* with all its good advice about simplifying, more times than they may have wanted to hear about it.

It may be that the best I can do is have the conversation, urge them to be generous, share whatever things matter to them, and let the rest go — perhaps some of it to others who have cared about me, and some of it quietly deposited in the recycling bin. It may also be that my simply releasing it all is a message in itself. "These things have served their purpose," T. S. Eliot writes in a line I've often had occasion to remember. "Let them be." And so I must, and will. I release them back into the stream of time, as a fly fisherman releases his catch. I have had the great pleasures and moments of learning they provided. Now I let my things go with gratitude and a prayer for those who stand downstream to receive them.

God of all provision, I thank you for the material blessings I have enjoyed in the time I've been given. May they bless others now, and may I be freed in releasing them to open my arms to a new life in you. Amen.

. . . Who from our mothers' arms has blessed us
on our way
With countless gifts of love. . . .

Leave-taking

Isaac sent them on their way, and they departed from him in peace.

GENESIS 26:31

Because I know I'm living out the final days of my life, I have a chance to say good-bye — a chance people don't get who go out suddenly by accidents or heart attacks. Hard as the good-byes are, I'm grateful for the time I'm given to say them.

It's a bit awkward to say them and keep on living, since none of us knows the day or the hour of my going. In my wakeful hours I imagine things I'd like to say to each of them who have shared my life in their very different ways. For one, there are still hurts to try to assuage, though forgiveness has been given and received; she needs a special tenderness to remember when I'm gone. For another, there are instructions: I count on her to manage many of the practical matters the closer family won't want to take care of, and she'll be glad for something to do in such a time. For another, there is reassurance, and for another — the wanderer — an appeal to reconnect in deeper ways with the family that will need him now.

I feel the need to reassure them that I'm not afraid. I trust God's word and love. I trust that I'm going to a new dimension of life, that I'll see them again in some new, larger, lightened, freed form of being, and that there will be laughter and recognition and rejoicing.

I feel the need to release them all with permission they may need from me: You'll do fine. You don't need to be afraid to go on with lives that will have less and less to do with me, or with preserving my memory. You don't need to worry about disloyalty in bringing a new person into the family in my place. Let yourselves be comforted. Let yourselves be blessed. Let yourselves grieve and then let go of grief and embrace your own adventures and the lives you've been given.

We've all been conditioned to think we can stay uninterruptedly in touch, so it's harder to imagine now than it used to be how final a real good-bye once was. When people left their homelands and traveled by ship to places where mail came every few months, if at all, waving good-bye must have felt something like death. Still, people chose to step aboard and choose new lives and take new risks. People left those they loved behind. They must have been a little better prepared for the last good-bye than most of us are now.

Jack Kerouac hasn't been a very reliable source of spiritual wisdom, but I do like what he said about good-byes: "What is that feeling when you're driving away from people and they recede on the plain till you see their specks dispersing? — it's the too-huge world vaulting us, and it's good-bye. But we lean forward to the next crazy venture beneath the skies." I want to go leaning forward. I want them to lean forward too, into the adventures that remain for them. I want my good-byes to come with a blessing and a nudge in that direction.

God, you are the source of all adventure. Lead each of us now into this new chapter of life, through and beyond death. Let our release of each other open our arms wide to welcome whatever comes next. Amen.

God be with you till we meet again. . . .

Full of Years

Abraham breathed his last and died in a good old age,
an old man and full of years. . . .

GENESIS 25:8

Years ago I read *How We Die* by Sherwin Nuland. I appreciated his candor about the sentimentalities we seize upon to protect ourselves from the hard parts of shedding this body and this life. About the notion of "death with dignity," he writes, "I have not often seen much dignity in the process by which we die." It's possible that giving up hope of a dignified death may open the way for a little wry humor and some final lessons in humility. There will be incontinence and sweaty sheets and help of the sort we don't want to need.

On dying of old age, Nuland's most memorable sentence is this one: "The very old do not succumb to disease — they implode their way into eternity." He goes on to explain how the body's systems shut down one by one, and to remind us that the "cause of death" doctors are required to provide is, in the case of old age, more complex than "congestive heart failure" or "pneumonia." If we are given a long life "full of years" and die, as so few now do, of "natural causes," we simply die of aging. Some of the parts wear out. But the notion of "imploding into eternity" makes me smile, and imagine that there are worse ways to go.

One of my favorite Rembrandt paintings is a portrait of an aged man entitled "An Old Jew." When I first saw it, I thought of the mysterious instruction in the Kabbalah: "Imagine that you are light." One way to think of the resurrected bodies we are promised is that we will live at a higher frequency — that the matter of which we are made will be something more like light. I imagined the old man imagining that he was light. The poem that came to me then comes back to me now, as I consider how I — and we all — will be changed.

An Old Jew
What he learned from Kabbalah:
"Imagine that you are light."

In a world of darkness
he has done that.

Wrapped in wool
as winter once again
closes over Amsterdam
and twilight gathers
in the afternoon,

he imagines light
parting flesh like cloud,

dissolving the wrinkled
weight of sorrow,
making the dry bones dance.

It is what he will become —
is becoming — as the dark descends.

As my body gets harder to move, my joints stiffer, my hearing
duller, my eyes dimmer, my appetite sketchier, I like imagining that I am light. I savor Jesus' mysterious, challenging word
to his disciples: "You are the light of the world." Light is what
we already are. Light is what we will become. I look forward
to the lightening.

*Prepare me, God, to be changed. Gather to yourself what
remains when these bones and flesh have finished their
good service. Thank you for the fullness of days I have been
given. May I enter eternity with delight. Amen.*

But 'ere my soul from earth remove,
O let me put Thine image on!

Body of Christ

Now you are the body of Christ, and individually members of it.

1 CORINTHIANS 12:27

The Amish consider the sick and the dying gifts to the community because they bring forth others' kindness. It's a consoling idea that the dying serve a purpose. I don't feel like much of a gift these days. Though the pastor visits, and people bring cards and flowers, I feel remote from and useless to the church I've loved for so many years. I used to show up at meetings to plan retreats and bring salads to potlucks and help prepare communion. I used to visit the sick. I used to reassure them, when I was the one standing by the bedside secure in my health, that they weren't forgotten, that we were praying for them, that they were still very much among us.

Now I know that the waters close behind us when we cease to show up, and that, though particular friends faithfully pray and visit, the remoteness is real. This sense of having left the church behind is one of many reminders that I am leaving others behind. I think of Jesus assuring the disciples that he goes to prepare a place for them. I hope and trust that he's prepared a place for me.

Every Sunday I affirm my belief in "the communion of saints," members of Christ's body both living and dead. I've visited two churches where the scope of that phrase came alive for me. At the Cathedral of St. Mary of the Angels in Los Angeles, tapestries running the length of the long sanctuary depict saints from every age in togas, bonnets, military gear, and martyrs' robes, all facing the altar along with the congregation. Among them, I realized that death is indeed only a temporary separation.

In St. Gregory of Nyssa Episcopal Church in San Francisco, a similar gathering is painted on a large panel that encircles the rotunda. It's a motley fellowship that includes not only St. Francis and St. Catherine of Siena and Saints Peter and Paul, but Emily Dickinson and Martin Luther King and Malcolm X and, I believe, a dancing bear. While some might find its wild and wide embrace offensive, I smile every time I visit there to think whom we might meet on the other side, and how surprised we may be. The painting testifies to the infinite mercy of a God who loves all creatures, knows our stories, and leads us in kindly light along our various paths.

I am a member of that body, whether or not I ever again gather with others inside a church. I will take my place in the great circle. I already pray from a new vantage point for those who remain, that they might be equipped for the global challenges they face, that they might be spared the worst of the wars and droughts and famines that afflict this ailing planet, and that they might contribute to its healing with a sturdy faith that will see them through.

In the course of seven years, every cell in our bodies dies and is replaced. But these dead cells are not lost but transformed, as matter turns to energy and bread to bone. When I die, this "too, too solid flesh" will melt, and I will be released into the light, and into the arms of the One who is with us always.

Loving God, enliven in me the hope of heaven and deepen my "conviction of things not seen." Help me to come willingly, in your good time, to take my place among those who have loved you faithfully and imperfectly, and to take with joy and confidence that last small step across the thin threshold that divides this world from the next. Amen.

Bread of life and cup of promise,
In this meal we all are one.
In our dying and our rising,
May your Kingdom come.

PRAYERS FOR THE FINAL DAYS

Loving God, help me accept this dying.
Help me live each day of it in trust,
remembering that your grace is sufficient
even for this stretch of the journey.

If it is your will even now to heal my body, I ask for healing.
If it is my time to release this life and enter into a new life
*   with you,*
deepen my trust that I can lie down in peace and
*   sleep each night*
in the safety of your arms,
that in life or death I am yours,
that you gather us all to yourself one by one
and bring us home.

*   *   *

I ask your blessing on this body in its brokenness.
I thank you for every delight it has given me,
and for the lessons I have learned from its pain,
for its fearful, wonderful, and intricate network
of nerves and rivers of blood,
for brain and heart, eyes and ears,
and hands now open before you
to receive whatever comes.

Touch me in my places of pain, and open me to your healing.
Connect me in this time to all who prepare for death.
I pray for them as others pray for me.

*   *   *

Teach me the discipline of full release.
Let me go lighter into the light.

*   *   *

Keep my heart open.
Let my pain not breed self-pity
nor my wakeful nights, discontent
nor others' health, envy.

*   *   *

Keep me curious, O Lord of life.
Let me learn what I can, even in this hard time, about
Patience
Acceptance
Trust
Humility
Gratitude
Resilience
Peace that passes understanding
and outlasts pain.

*   *   *

Even now, O God, help me choose life.
Help me to live each day of it in love,
to rest in complete trust,
to wake into a new kind of hope,
to enjoy what pleasures come in the course of these days,
to be as grateful as I am sorrowful for the life I am
preparing to leave.

*   *   *

Bless the conversations these days bring.
Keep them honest and kind.
Let me lay aside all pretense.
Keep me open to others' needs,
aware that my dying is also their loss.
Let me not lose my laughter.
Let me go generously, even joyfully,
into that "good night" that opens into resurrection morning.

* * *

God, I join with all who are dying of this disease.
I ask that you lighten their pain and mine.
Give them, and give me, a strong sense of your presence.
Bring them and bring me healing sleep in the long nights.
Guide their doctors, and mine, in every intervention.
Hold their families, and mine, near your heart as they
    face this going.
Help them, and help me, receive each remaining day
    in gratitude.
Make their going, and mine, gentle, without struggle,
a swift passing into your marvelous light.

* * *

When I feel entrapped in this body,
when pain leaves me no hiding place,
when frustration turns to rage,
Jesus, be near me.

When others' kindness only irritates,
when food and drink turn to ash,
when old resentments fester,
Jesus, be near me.

When every encounter exhausts me,
when doubts gather and darken my mind,
when all desire for prayer dries up,
Jesus, be near me.

Be near me and comfort me.
Be near me and lead me to still waters.
Be near me and breathe on me, breath of God.

*   *   *

God of all healing, preserve those who love me
from fatigue, as they lay aside their needs for mine;
from resentment, as they face the realities of loss;
from contention, as they share in the duties of caregiving;
from anxiety, as they witness the course this illness takes;
from fear, as they ponder what cannot be predicted;
from despair, as they face this death, and their own.

Comfort them when they are sad.
Encourage them when they are afraid.
Send them companions when they need help.
Make them wise stewards of their own life and health.
Help them accept what they must
and enjoy what they can
and, curling into the shadow of your great wings,
find their rest in you.

*   *   *

Creator God, sustain in me a spirit of thanksgiving
        for every day
you give me on this beautiful earth.
Let me notice the "greenly spirits" of trees
and the beauty of the moon in its waxing and waning.
Even now, teach me to be amazed.

*   *   *

Time, like an ever-rolling stream,
Bears all our years away;
They fly, forgotten, as a dream
Dies at the opening day.

                    (From "O God, Our Help in Ages Past")

Grant me the energy and discernment
to tell the stories that will help others along the way,
and to let those that would not be helpful be forgotten.

Let me seek not so much to be remembered
as to leave a legacy of love,
cast abroad and taking root
wherever the wind of your Spirit bears it.

Erase from the memories of those who love me
all angry words, hasty judgments, thoughtless moments.
Let them remember me as and when they need to.

May my life, remembered, be a testimony to your faithfulness.
May my life, forgotten, be hidden with Christ,
transformed and perfected by his infinite mercy.

*   *   *

"Be Thou my vision, O Lord of my heart."

As I relinquish this vast and beautiful world, O God,
prepare me for a wider one,
illumined by the light of your countenance.
As I bid good-bye to all I have known in this life,
Help me look back on its blessings with gratitude,
on its losses with acceptance,
on its suffering with compassion,
on its mysteries with awe.
In each dear face I love, show me
your own dear self, indwelling, at home
within and among us.
Amen.

Made in the USA
Columbia, SC
23 June 2021

40905298R00093